THE PREDATOR PARADOX

THE PREDATOR PARADOX

Ending the War with Wolves,
Bears, Cougars, and Coyotes

JOHN A. SHIVIK

BEACON PRESS, BOSTON

BEACON PRESS
Boston, Massachusetts
www.beacon.org

Beacon Press books
are published under the auspices of
the Unitarian Universalist Association of Congregations.

17 16 15 14   8 7 6 5 4 3 2 1

This book is printed on acid-free paper that meets the uncoated paper
ANSI/NISO specifications for permanence as revised in 1992.

Text design and composition by Wilsted & Taylor Publishing Services

Author's note: This book was composed entirely outside of and independently
from other duties and job responsibilities I have in life. It expresses my own
personal and scientific musings and nothing within it should be construed as
being representative of opinions or policies of the Utah Division of Wildlife
Resources or other agencies.

LIBRARY OF CONGRESS CATALOGING-IN-PUBLICATION DATA

Shivik, John A.
  The predator paradox : ending the war with wolves, bears, cougars, and
coyotes / by John A. Shivik.
      pages cm
  Includes bibliographical references and index.
  ISBN 978-0-8070-8496-0 (hardcover : alk. paper)
  ISBN 978-0-8070-8497-7 (ebook)
  1. Predation (Biology) —North America. 2. Predatory animals—Control—
North America. 3. Human-animal relationships—North America. I. Title.
  QL758.S54 2014
  591.5'3—dc23   2013045410

For my son, Fox

The prey must have the predator,
just as the predator needs the prey.
One without the other eventually
becomes something less. The wolf
becomes the dog. The deer becomes
a cow. And what does man become?

—**LARRY MARCHINGTON**
    Address to Keepers of the Hunting Spirit
    Melbourne, Australia
    June 1991

CONTENTS

PART I. THE WAR

CHAPTER 1   THE BATTLEFIELD   3

CHAPTER 2   PREDATORS, PEOPLE, AND PREY
Impacts and Interactions   24

CHAPTER 3   FOOD
An Inseparable Connection   42

CHAPTER 4   PERCEPTIONS THAT FUEL THE PARADOX   51

PART II. DÉTENTE

CHAPTER 5   THE PHENOMENON OF FRIGHT
Disruptive Stimuli   69

CHAPTER 6   PERSONALITY AND PEER PRESSURE   89

CHAPTER 7   OF SPIKED DOUGHNUTS AND
TURBO-CHARGED FLAGGING
Testing Aversive Stimuli   102

CHAPTER 8   CLOSE, BUT NOT TOO CLOSE
Altering Territories   121

CHAPTER 9   ANIMAL HUSBANDRY
Sometimes It's About Money, Sometimes It's Not   134

CHAPTER 10   THE POWER OF EMOTION AND
THE NEED FOR KNOWLEDGE   146

ACKNOWLEDGMENTS   169
APPENDIX   172
NOTES   175
INDEX   189

PART I

THE WAR

CHAPTER 1

THE BATTLEFIELD

Spanish Fork, Utah's glass and steel reflected the red morning light, sparkling like scattered rubies. On the other side of the aircraft, under the rising sun, stretched a stark, dark contrast of wilderness terrain. The pilot navigated over the narrow edge: the interface of wilderness and humanity.

The slopes, rocky and rugged, stood too tall and steep to be colonized by people, but the asphalt and concrete constructions of humanity to the west were equally challenging to invasion by wild animals. The view from the helicopter created the illusion that the boundary of wilderness was as razor sharp and distinct as the heights of the Wasatch.

If one looked closer, however, intrusions became evident; the edge dulled and blurred. On a ridgeline, ski tracks ran down the face. Figure eights wove in and out of an avalanche chute. The interlopers had managed to dance down the virgin snowfield without being swallowed by it.

Where humans broke trails in, animals loped their way out. Coyotes enjoyed an advantage from the intrusion, as snowmobiles created firm paths through the depths of Utah's "greatest snow on earth." Paw prints on packed powder led to town, where dispersing canids could find a snack of domestic house cat. Cougars followed deer that were drawn to the rosebuds of lush suburbs. When the bears awoke, they would find their way to apple trees on the edge of town. The human-wildland interface below me wasn't a razor-edge solid border but a porous ecotone.

Our machine flew over moose—one, two, three. A mother with her calf—four, five. Number six, reduced to a mat of hair and jumble of bones, the hide chewed, processed, and defecated in adjacent scats. This was the reason for our flight: reports of wolves just outside of the suburban sprawl. We found a carcass, tracks, and evidence, but no proof strong enough to identify true wolf from feral dog or hybrid.

The southwest corner of wolf-range in Wyoming was barely one hundred miles away, only a morning's walk for a wolf. We did not yet know if it was a jaunt or sortie, or if wolves had actually reestablished themselves and bred in Utah, but the line between humans and predators was blurring. It was long past time to ask the question: Could or would we learn to live with mammalian predators as close neighbors? Between past and future were a myriad of considerations.

Beginning in the 1600s, European settlers came to the New World, bringing their God-given mandate to tame the wilderness. In addition, they carried within them generations of myth, fear, and violent reaction to predators such as the wolf. By the turn of the twentieth century, agricultural heavy-handedness had imposed nearly two hundred years of ecological emptiness, and expanses of the American West had become devoid of top predators. We had forgotten in a very deep way what it meant to have among us animals that made their livings eating other sentient things. By the 1950s, largely through actions of federal trappers, we had killed off nearly every wolf and grizzly bear in the contiguous United States and had similarly decimated black bear, cougar, and even coyote populations in some places.[1]

Soon after the time of the 1962 publication of *Silent Spring*, the pendulum of public opinion swung back, carrying with it a crying Indian, the Endangered Species Act, and Earth Day. In barely a generation, many North Americans had developed a sense of environmentalism and a depth of ecology that lacked such a concept as "varmints" (except perhaps humans). They wanted coyotes, bears, cougars, and wolves to exist. Even more, they wanted people to stop killing them.

I was studying wildlife biology as the field grew rapidly and diversified. The discipline had been utilitarian, hook-and-bullet, strictly about game management, but all of a sudden it was adding elements of pure and deep ecology. As a graduate student in the 1990s, I captured, radio-collared, and followed coyotes because I believed that studying predators would lead us on the path toward coexistence. An MS, a PhD, and dozens of students and studies later, I am still sorting out the paradox of desperately wanting to conserve and increase populations of the animals that we spent so much time and energy exterminating.

In North America, we think differently about predators than we used to, especially on the burgeoning, suburbanizing coasts. It puts us humans on a collision course with remaining and rebounding populations of wolves, bears, cougars, and coyotes. The rapid sprawl of civilization forces the issue: Is there anywhere else for predators to go if they can't live on humanity's doorstep? Are there options that would allow us to have carnivores in our kingdom while we protect our livestock, property, and people? Finally, who is going to jump in the fray between people and predators and end the feud?

"My God, they're beautiful," Lynne Gilbert-Norton gasped, seeing a coyote for the first time.

The coyote was a few yards away, on the other side of a fence, standing broadside to us. Its black-furred back faded to tan, then brushed into the red that lined the outer edges of its pointed ears, which flittered up like furry pyramids focusing sound. The yellow fires of its eyes did not look away from Lynne in deference, but peered back, insubordinately, into hers. Black lines, like Cleopatra's eyeliner, ran from their corners. Superfluously painted and defiant, the coyote's eyes had the duality of menace and allure.

Lynne, of the University of Exeter, had been sent to study something uniquely American. She acknowledged that coyotes weren't animals normally studied by her colleagues and professors. "I'm a psychologist, a Brit," she said. "I read, but still don't feel like I know much about coyotes."

"Hardly anyone sees a coyote close up like this," I said. "Even Americans." I prodded, "So you're lucky. The question is, What are you going to do with them?"

The issue, of course, was much more complicated than my innocent inquiry suggested. I was asking Lynne to find out how to live with animals that have no qualms about eating our livestock, our property, even us. How do we outsmart them on their own playing field? I knew it was going to take more than one or two biologists or a few grandfathers of conservation biology to find the answers. It would also require an army of young diverse minds, everyone from foreigners to farm boys.

More than a hundred coyotes responded to my question. Waves of rapid ululations and high-pitched barks and yips filled the air. Lynne froze, uncertain. It sounded like the home team had scored in a nearby football stadium.

Above us stood nature's castellation, the raw edges of the Bear River Range. The United States had towering castles and cathedrals as did England, but ours were geological. Everywhere the new world collided with the ancient. The road leading to our location weaved between fields, one flooded with water and white-faced ibis, others yielding young stalks of corn. An inconspicuous blue and white sign marked state property, "Utah State University Millville Wildlife Research Center," alongside a humble plaque reading, "United States Department of Agriculture, Wildlife Services, Predator Research Facility," indicating the collaborative federal pens and buildings sharing the land.

The Predator Research Facility was crammed between rugged desert and high country mountaintops, between the fantasy of apple pie America and the reality of the abattoirs of the nearby town of Hyrum, Utah. It was wedged between university professors' tentative search for truth and Utah's religious roots in dominating nature and demanding that the desert bloom. For Lynne and her fellow students, it was also the base camp for a journey. She had no idea of the significance of the research that she'd signed up for, or how a simple little predator would change her life.

❦ ❦ ❦

Charismatic song dogs to some, vile varmints to others, the coyote is our most widespread North American meat eater. Typically considered the second-class cousin to the wolf, coyotes were confined to the American southwest at the time of European arrival. As hedgerows, irrigation, crops, and humans displaced the larger and less compromising wolf, coyotes filled the void. Seizing the opportunity, they became a continental predator, and are currently found from Central America to Alaska.[2] Today, coyotes are seen, or their effects felt, by citizens of every state except Hawaii. Drawn by both cat food and cats as food, they are literally at our kitchen doors.[3]

Varying in form and habit across their range, coyotes as a species seem infinitely adaptable, at home in cities, towns, tall mountains, and open deserts. They tend to be smaller in the southern part of their range, weighing perhaps twenty pounds as adults, and larger in the north, nearing forty pounds. The animal known as the eastern coyote is the giant of the species, sometimes weighing more than fifty pounds, rivaling the size of a well-fed German shepherd.[4]

In Native American traditions dating back to the Aztecs, the coyote has been assigned a variety of personalities and responsibilities. From a creator of the earth, to mischief maker, to utter fool, he is the Native American Robin Goodfellow, and his spirit and symbolism are equally protean. Even within the pantheon of the Aztecs, the coyote had many faces. *Tezcatlipoca* would transform himself into a coyote and trot ahead to warn travelers of robbers or other dangers in front of them. In contrast, *Huehuecoyotl*, the Old Coyote, was a nefarious mischief-maker.[5]

Farther to the north, Native American tribes had similar impressions of the coyote: godlike in cunning, but with a humanlike sense of morality. The demigod of coyote was said to be responsible for the presence of fish in the Klamath River and for giving the bison, with a kick of dust, its poor eyesight. The coyote brought fire to the people as the Native American Prometheus, but he was also their Azrael, bringing death. When the just and worthy died, their souls went to a good place, but the wicked were reborn into coyotes.[6]

The legends, much like the animal, changed with the arrival of newcomers. The Spanish adopted the Aztec word, *coyotl*, which morphed over time, the final "l" becoming an "e." Subtle changes of meaning crept in. In Steinbeck's *The Pearl*, Kino and Juana's only son is named *Coyotito*, little coyote, and in the Spanish of the time the term referred to the last child produced by a family, magnifying the tragedy of his demise.[7] The coyote of today's Mexican vernacular is a shady character who smuggles people across the desert. The coyote operates in both shadow and light: it is never entirely clear whether he is beneficent or malevolent.

The folklore accurately assesses the scrappy, multifaceted essence of the biological coyote as well. Coyotes sometimes live in packs and drag down large prey, but other times they subsist solitarily on field mice. The coyote is a character; even to the short-sleeved, white button-down-shirted statisticians of the National Agricultural Statistics Service. Yearly reports estimate that coyotes are responsible for 60.5 percent of all sheep losses to predation, representing an estimated $18.3 million in total losses.[8] Stemming from a long and antagonistic history, the tongue-in-cheek advertisement "Eat lamb—20,000 coyotes can't be wrong," continues to grace the bumpers of many pickup trucks in the American West.

The object of many a coyote's appetitive affections is the domestic sheep, a dumbed down version of the mouflon, which resembles the bighorn of North America. Our sheep originated in Mesopotamia 11,000 years ago, near the confluence of the Tigris and Euphrates.[9] By 1000 AD, Spain was a major player in sheep production. It was only natural for the beasts, which even sailed with Columbus, to expand across the American West. Predatory defenses are largely nonexistent in the domestic sheep. They are awkward and slow, like wooly dinner with hooves. As biologists often put it, "Sheep are born. Then they spend the rest of their lives looking for a place to die."

Domestic sheep, especially lambs, are not much of a challenge for a coyote, which bears an uncanny resemblance to the closely related golden jackal, which would have eaten the domestic sheep's ancestors on the Arabian Peninsula. The ongoing battle between humans and predators started even before our religious divisions did. Over the ages, fear and loathing of all predators has become as natural to us as growing food has.

Ironically, the urban population centers of the coasts have tended to be blissfully unaware of the deep-seated resentment and conflict on the rural prairies. Until recently, only livestock producers felt the majority of the economic and emotional impact of the pesky predator. Although coyotes may now have a certain symbolism and mysticism for newcomers to the West, management in rural areas has been a long, intensive, and passionate tradition, inherited through generations, like a hundred-years' war.

And a war it has been. As sheep production in the United States was peaking in the 1940s, demobilization caused a surplus of military-trained pilots with the skill, fortitude, and willingness to fly at low levels. It is expected that the technological advances of war would be incorporated into other elements of life. Armed with shotguns and hanging out the back of a Piper Cub, hunters could experience the thrill of the chase while minimizing the danger of low-level flying. At least no one was shooting back.

Aerial hunting, as it is called, remains a zealously embraced tool of Wildlife Services, the branch of the United States Department of Agriculture that has stepped up to control our interstate predators. Critics often refer to it as "aerial gunning," because raining bullets from the sky onto coyotes caught in the middle of a vast snowfield doesn't sound like hunting. Body counts can be phenomenal; from 2001 to 2007, a total of 252,713 animals were taken from the air. Of those, coyotes accounted for a majority, 210,306.[10] The agency's summary from 2008 reported that 50,846 animals were lethally removed from sixteen states using fixed wing aircraft (30,537 animals) and helicopters (20,309). Coyotes were the most numerous of the species taken, with a death toll of 36,454, but the total included wolves (444), red fox (140), feral hogs (13,620), and bobcats (188).[11]

The technology gives the impression of ease, but even so there is an art to the method, which relies on more than eagle-eyed pilots and steady gunners. Crews wait for snow. Coyotes contrast with the white landscape, which makes them possible to spot from long distances. They can't escape the evidence of their tracks. Once they have been spotted, air strikes commence. Today, coyotes are hunted from the air in twenty-eight states using seventy-four aircraft. Because chases occur at very low altitudes and at near-stall speeds, the practice is dangerous for humans. Thirty-six accidents, causing ten fatalities, occurred between 1979 and 2007.[12]

The use of aerial hunting grew after President Nixon, possibly the most environmental of all US presidents, banned the use of toxicants on public ranges in 1972.[13] Before Nixon, wide-scale use of baits and carcasses laced with Compound 1080 or strychnine made it possible to kill far more coyotes (as well as any other scavenging species) across large swaths of landscape. During the 1950s, although coyotes were ranging east and north, the animals were extirpated from the Edwards Plateau of Texas, and the use of widely distributed indiscriminate poisons made it possible to keep them out. When the ban was instituted, Animal Damage Control (as Wildlife Services was known then) state directors panicked, but in short order they found other technologies, such as airplanes, that kept the body counts high.

◗ ◗ ◗

As in all wars, new technologies enable killing with increased efficiency and brutality, so it was natural that our zest for conquering each other would spill over to affect other species. It wasn't anything new in North American attitude or thought. Wolves had long been targeted for extermination—and results achieved—in the old country. Even with the limited tools of earlier times, humans had eliminated wolves from Scotland by 1684, Ireland by 1770, Denmark by 1772, and Bavaria, Poland, and France by 1847, 1900, and 1927, respectively.[14]

After the Civil War, the US government had new tools of destruction and newfound strength in its federal bureaucracy. Great federal juggernauts often have humble beginnings, and our current system of predator control was not created in a day.[15] In 1886, the USDA created the Branch of Economic Ornithology and Mammalogy when scientists concluded something more than scarecrows was needed to reduce bird damage. In a foreshadowing of the technique of reinvention that the agency would use to grow—or survive—the name was changed four years later to the Division of Ornithology and Mammalogy. This became the Division of Biological Survey in 1896, then the Bureau of Biological Survey in 1905. Its mission crept accordingly, with rodent control added to the list of responsibilities in 1913. With a humble budget of $125,000 in 1915, predator control began. This agency of singular purpose, but fickleness of name, became the Division of Predatory

Animal and Rodent Control (PARC) in 1924. Long before current euphemisms were created, the Eradication Methods Laboratory was established in Albuquerque, New Mexico, in 1920. However, the year that heralds the transition from mission creep to federal takeover of state management of predators was 1931, with passage of the Animal Damage Control Act.

Could the act's framers have known how the federal stake in predator management would grow? Typically, in accordance with the Tenth Amendment of the US Constitution, powers not dictated to the federal government are reserved by individual states. Thus, most wildlife such as deer, elk, rabbits, beavers, and all manner of furbearers and other species are managed exclusively by each state, while interstate and international peregrinations of birds came under federal control through the Migratory Bird Treaty Act, justified under the Constitution's commerce clause. Likewise with the Endangered Species Act. The oldest, richest, and most powerful of federal agencies intruding into states' sovereignty over wildlife, however, remains the one created in 1931 solely to kill animals. It is now known as Wildlife Services.

Name changes, bureaucratic jockeying, and growth continued through the years, but as a *spiritus mundi* of environmental concern developed, so did controversy over systematic, government-sponsored destruction of wildlife. A panel formed in 1963 examined rodent and predator control activities. Its findings make up the Leopold Report, coauthored by A. Starker Leopold, son of the famous father of wildlife management, Aldo Leopold.[16] The panel strongly criticized the predator control activities of what had come to be known as the Section of Predator and Rodent Control. The agency ducked, dodged, and renamed itself Wildlife Services (for the first time) but pursued little fundamental change in its activities. The next notable investigation into the agency culminated in the Cain Report in 1972.[17] It made a number of recommendations, including this: "All existing toxic chemicals should be removed from registration and use for Federal operational predator control," and this: "Federal and state legislation should make the shooting from aircraft of wildlife, including predators and game animals, illegal except under exceptional circumstances." In response, the agency changed its name again, in 1974 acquiring the black-hat appellation representing all that is evil to modern day predator advocates: Animal Damage Control, or ADC.

Everyone agreed that it was not a good fit. The agency that was sworn to kill predators was housed within the Fish and Wildlife Service, which administered the oppositely envisioned Endangered Species Act. Irreconcilable differences were acknowledged, and by 1985 ADC was transferred back to the US Department of Agriculture under the Animal and Plant Health Inspection Service (APHIS), an agency better known for veterinarians who inspect the meat supply, and for officials who enforce the Animal Welfare Act. The retransformation was complete in 1997, when the agency once again became Wildlife Services—drawing cynical criticism that it was simply trying to shrug off the bad press of previous decades by changing its letterhead instead of its activities.

▼ ▼ ▼

Predator management in the United States primarily means flying helicopters, setting cyanide ejectors, hiding traps, and using ambush and sniper tactics to slay animals. Indeed, the longest war carried out by the US government, beginning with a federal appropriation in 1914, is our war with our mammalian predators. The death toll is tremendous: 84,584 wolves, coyotes, bears, and lions were terminated by the Department of Agriculture, Wildlife Services, in 2011 alone.[18] At 365, wolf deaths amounted to exactly one wolf a day for the year. Including raccoons, ungulates, birds, and all other species, a total of 3,779,024 animals were killed in 2011, according to the agency's tabulation.[19] That was a slow year; 4,997,172 animals were killed in 2008, and 4,120,295 in 2009.[20] With such numbing casualty figures, modern predator management looks like a war not only with predators, but one with nature itself.

The list of species and species assemblages killed (intentionally or not) by agents is several pages long and includes many innocents and questionable species, such as the American avocet, white-winged dove, eastern bluebird, rustic bunting, northern cardinal, harlequin duck, Say's phoebe, desert cottontail rabbit, gopher snake, tundra swan, and downy woodpecker. It is 326 entries long (see appendix).

In a war, there will be collateral damage.

❦ ❦ ❦

Coyotes, for their part, are just doing what is natural for them. They seek places to make a living and raise their young. They always have more pups than will survive so that when there is a death, and a slot opens, there will be another animal there to fill it. If there is enough food and space, their numbers swell exponentially. With an average of six pups per breeding pair each year, coyotes have prodigious reproductive potential. Two have six. Two years later, each female could produce six more. Six, times six, times six. Modeling the potential growth of a coyote population is awe-inspiring.

The first population models calculated in the 1970s by USDA biologist Guy Connolly, and since rerun and revised with equivalent results, show the species' Lazarus-like ability to rebound from massive killings. Connolly's calculations indicate that more than 70 percent of coyotes have to be removed from an area every year for several years to bring about population reduction.[21]

Like rats, cheat-grass, kudzu, raccoons, white-tailed deer, ragweed, and Russian thistle, coyotes generate a yearly overabundance of replacements. This list of the earth's expanding species, the reproductive overachievers, is collectively assigned the appellation "weed species" by keen observers such as David Quammen.[22] The species are called weeds, of course, because they pop up like dandelion heads in what we want to be a maintenance-free Garden of Eden. Where are humans in the list? Our long lives and reproductive ability is astounding. From 1990 to 2000, the United States population grew by 32.7 million, a whopping 13.2 percent in ten years.[23] We are not that different from coyotes.

The term "weed," or its animal equivalent "varmint," begs the questions: Is nature supposed to be an even lawn without competition and variation? Are humans different than other animals and rightfully set apart from nature? Who should be expected to altruistically forgo reproduction, limit their range and not alter the environment to suit themselves and their progeny? Is one worse than the other—a pregnant woman painting a nursery or a coyote digging a den?

How different people approach or answer those questions tells a lot about how widely fundamental human values can differ. Some people would be offended that the questions are even posed. Others are smugly confident in their own reply. Some are entrenched on one side or the other, but many struggle on the uncertain no-man's-land between.

Ghostly mist hung over the lowest flats of Utah's Cache Valley. It condensed on long-dormant stalks of flowers that had become dried packets of hopeful seeds. A white van with government license plates emerged and passed through the gates of the Predator Research Facility. The van swung left, parking in front of the terra-cotta and gray cinder block office building.

Driven by the dean of Utah State University's College of Natural Resources, the van was filled with congressional staff from Washington, DC. The dean had the notion that if the aides saw the potential and need for such a facility, Senator Hatch would too, and federal funds would result. The staffers pressed their faces against the van's glass like schoolchildren, expectant breath steaming the windows as they studied the moonlike landscape, the air colder than ice, the snow as dry as dust. The low sun, straining to rise over the Bear River Range, drew long, contrasting shadows on what moments before was only white on white. The air was so clear that it hurt to look into the distance, and the sky above the mist was infinity blue. Wearing suits and ties or black business slacks or skirts, staffers piled out of the side door, pushing and bumping off each other. Their breath steamed in the cold air, but no one spoke. They formed a line, fidgeting with phones in their pockets but leaving them hidden. They focused instead on the white-capped mountains that hovered above the fog.

Dean Fee Busby slammed the van door and a wail emanated from the mist to the east. At the sound, the great power-brokers stopped in place, mouths open, eyes darting. The senator's staff, frozen like statues, had to be thawed, prodded, and herded into the building so the tour could begin.

The Predator Research Facility was the brainchild of Dr. Fred Knowlton, known to many biologists from the 1970s to the '90s as "Mr. Coyote." Fred received his PhD in 1964, and in 1972 was assigned to what was then the Denver Wildlife Research Center's collaborative field station at Utah State University. In 1973 he spied one hundred acres of land, only five miles from the university, where he could construct observation buildings, kennels, and labs.

There was little money to build, but Fred was exceedingly frugal and clever as a coyote in bringing his dream to life. He was able to build an impressive facility with very little money. The downside of this approach: he built a large facility using very little money. He had applied the labor of biologists using miles of surplus scrap rods to create eight-foot ersatz fence posts. Stenciled lettering on tractors and the presence of a Korean War–vintage road grader indicated the equipment had previous lives as property of Hill Air Force Base. Nothing was thrown away. What was considered a "mound of junk" by research biologists and students was a "resource pile" to Fred. An even modest injection of funds could greatly improve the infrastructure.

After introductions and an overview of the facility, Senator Hatch's staff piled back into the van, where the station leader kneeled backward in the front passenger seat and pointed out features of the facility, as if he were giving a tour of homes of the rich and famous. All eyes were glued to the windows, no texts were read or sent.

"There is nothing like it anywhere," the station leader spouted enthusiastically. "What we have here is a full staff—the best staff that has ever been assembled in the history of the planet—all dedicated to learning about predators. We have students that come here from all over the world. We are developing methods that will help resolve conflicts between humans and predators. We are trying to help people, but if we do it right, we will help coyotes too. And not only coyotes . . . wolves, bears, cougars . . . all predators."

"Will coyotes—I mean, if you don't do anything—go extinct?" a staffer asked innocently. The others shuffled in their seats. Some nodded, some cocked their heads inquisitively.

"No," he chuckled. "In fact, coyotes are probably one of the most successful carnivores out there. They live everywhere from South America up through Alaska. They'll be here long after humans probably." He turned to the driver, the dean, and whispered and pointed directions. They drove through a trench; snow was plowed a few feet high on either side of the sandy road.

Another staffer stated more confidently, "I read that most of the problem is because we are moving into their homes."

"Hmmmm." He considered the point carefully. "In part, maybe. But we are also inviting them into ours. This valley would be a dry-grass desert if it weren't for people." There were trees everywhere. In summer, Cache Valley is a lush Eden of orchards and farm fields. "We irrigate, plant crops and trees that provide cover and food for deer and rodents and rabbits. That attracts coyotes. What we do makes life better for us, but it also ends up making life better for coyotes. That's why they are turning up in cities, Central Park. We aren't just invading nature, these guys are bringing nature to us. Our job is to figure out what to do about it."

Indeed, the significance of human action on the landscape is much greater than just the point-source plopping down of a house. Humans create a plethora of food, cover, and habitat. It is difficult to think of the American West in a nascent, pristine state, without the human touch. We divert streams and rivers to lower the peaks of spring floods and to dribble water through the droughts of fall. Our garbage, bird feeders, and pet food bowls sustain the lowest rungs on the food ladder. What one species does on the landscape can alter the entire composition of the plant and animal communities there: after we build the prey base, the predators come. Bears sleep under decks in the Lake Tahoe area and coyotes stroll across parks in urban Chicago. Cougars follow deer that invaded to browse on rose hips and wolves lope through calving pastures.

The packed van weaved through curves, passing near pens. Some coyotes, fluffy and comfortable in the cold, rested calmly on their shade shelters. They curled up on the meter-high tables with their tails brushed over their snouts. A few raised one eyelid and then went back to sleep. Others were already wide awake, running the length of the fence silently, not barking as a dog would, despite their Latin name, *Canis latrans*, meaning "barking dog." A few stalked the vehicle intently, as if they were following blind bison across the valley. Some pranced at the edge of the fence and raised their snouts and sniffed at the air. Still others backed away to the point in their pen most distant from the access road and huddled, concealed in a long shadow, eyeing the visitors diffidently.

The van swept along a two-mile loop as the station leader

pointed to a broken bit of fence here, or noted the dream of a new and better captive-animal habitat there, until they arrived again at the main office parking lot. Staffers poured out and followed the station leader into the shop section of the lab building.

Displayed prominently on the back wall were dozens of medieval-looking capture devices, beefy metal springs and unfathomable mechanisms with ruthless jaws. Everyone winced, imagining the horrors of the hardware as if they had stepped into Torquemada's dungeon.

"You get the point," the station leader said as he stopped in front of the wall. "This is the state of the art of wildlife management right now. Centuries-old technology."

He pulled a coyote trap off of the wall. "Here."

He nonchalantly cocked the mechanism and placed it on the bench before them. "This is just the beginning," he said calmly, then pressed the round pan down with his hand. The jaws slammed shut on his fingers. Those in the front row jumped. One person squeaked like a mouse and nearly dropped her clipboard.

The guide continued calmly: "What I mean is, compare this type of trap with older kinds." He held up the cold metal; it was firmly clamped around his fingers. "There are padded jaws here," he said, pointing with his free hand, drawing his finger across the edge of the jaws. "Coil springs, an offset—a gap—in the jaws, so there is actually pressure, but room for my fingers or an animal's toes." He lowered the trap to the floor and used the balls of his feet to press two levers and release the tension on the springs. "Short chain with a shock-absorber, a swivel here. Trust me, I wouldn't put my hand in some of those bad boys." He nodded toward the wall, where six-inch-wide toothed jaws and monstrous springs dangled menacingly on the pegboard. "We can do better with the technology we have."

They continued their inspection, stopping at a poster with three sections of text accompanied by pictures on glossy four-by-five foot paper. The title read "Alternative Methods and Non-Lethal Techniques for Managing Predation." Faces of wolves and bears appeared between the blocks of text. Photos showed what looked like red flags from the lot of a car dealership strung in front of a fence line, presumably to frighten wolves away from cows.

"Look." He palmed the front of the poster, lowering his voice. A few in the front row studied his fingers for evidence of trap damage, but saw none. "Every convenience store has motion sensors and automatically opening doors. There are security cameras and laser scanners and data systems. We aren't talking rocket science here. We just want to advance the science past the fallback position of metal springs and gunpowder."

"Time," the dean said, looking up from the itinerary. "Thank you for showing us around this amazing place." There was applause, handshaking, and an expressed wish among the hosts that the visit would result in increased funding for the university and research station.

The visitors left the building and dispersed around the lot. Cameras came out, staffers dashed in every direction. They took photos of the coyote statue at the gate, the mountains in the distance, and the station leader standing in the deep, soft snow, fluffy and pure. "Thanks for making the trip," he said. On cue, nearly one hundred coyotes raised their voices in wild harmony, sending the staffers off with the song of the West ringing in their ears.

❥ ❥ ❥

Lynne Gilbert-Norton knew little of American politics, senators, and funding, and had a short time to learn. She certainly hadn't paid attention to the tours and other such goings-on at the Predator Research Facility. Dutifully, she focused on the questions at hand. First, she had to survive in a foreign culture. The locals spoke a sort of English, but that was where the similarity stopped.

"What I'd give for just the bog-standard Tetley, the little round ones," she pined, unprepared for American ignorance about tea. "And microwaves to boil water in? Ludicrous. One needs a proper kettle to make tea."

These were minor annoyances. She knew the focus needed to be on organizing the few months she would have to complete the required amount of research for her MS from the University of Exeter. Great minds had been studying coyotes for years, but so many questions remained: How do you know when a coyote will act on hunger or curiosity, or retreat in fear? How could that fear be harnessed to keep coyotes from attacking sheep? How was a young psychologist, who had never seen a coyote before, supposed to figure it out?

Delays were frustrating. New pens were being constructed, and there was an ever-present need to assist the animal-care staff. The station buzzed with activity and interpersonal strife. The staff demanded her help in caring for the animals and cleaning and raking. An overwhelming number of duties and ideas pulled at her. Lynne's advisors in England had cast her across the Atlantic and left it up to her. A month into her placement, she had nothing to show but a vague plan of action. The PhD station leader rapidly fired questions and suggestions, but Lynne didn't know which ones to catch, ride, or duck from.

Somewhere in the middle of the coyote pen before her, between a few clumps of high grass, were buckets that needed removing. Graduate students were at the bottom of the staff food chain, so it was pointless to make an argument about being sent on the errand. She also didn't want to get on the bad side of the facility manager, a woman who had a reputation for terrorizing newcomers. Lynne felt particularly in the gunsights, probably because she was a foreigner.

Lynne worried that she had a hell of a lot to accomplish, as she kicked away the stones on the threshold. Having no choice, she unchained the pen's gate and twisted up on the rod that anchored it into the concrete slab at the base. She swung the door wide.

Sighing, Lynne rested her arm on a crossbar and looked into the two-and-a-half acre, wedge-shaped pen before her. Supposedly there were two coyotes somewhere in the tall grass. She paused, turned, and huffed before stepping back out of the pen to get a pin stick, an implement a little over a yard long fashioned from one-quarter-inch reinforcement bar. It had a curled handle on one end and a Y-shaped split at the other. The forked end was wrapped with multiple layers of electrical tape as padding. Lynne had watched staff corner coyotes before, then use the aptly named device to press the animal to the ground by its neck. Once the coyote was pinned, the brave technician would ease his hand behind its head and grip fast, pulling the skin so tightly away from its snout that the animal was forced to smile. Having heard war stories of handling gone awry—the bites on the nose, the scars on arms—Lynne had sworn off any such risky activity, but she figured the pin stick was bad mojo to a coyote and a useful symbol of authority in a pen. They were predators, but she was human—the boss. They had to know that.

Two coyotes materialized about one hundred yards from her. Having found a vantage point, they stood and stared, showing a keen interest in the invader's activities.

Her back to the exit, Lynne walked into the pen, cutting the corner and angling toward the west side of the enclosure. Swinging the pin stick next to her, she decidedly put one foot in front of the other. Forward.

She strolled down the fence line and considered the contrast between this place and Devon, England. Here there was dry air and deep blue sky, and mountains rose before and behind her. The other students said that they felt like expatriates in Utah, too. The government, they told her, was dominated and run unabashedly by members of the Mormon faith known chiefly for its members' aversion to alcohol and coffee. People were all so different. She tapped the link of the fence with the end of the pin stick and stared at the ground as she walked.

The pen was a little more than 160 yards long and 125 yards across at the wide end. Its narrow apex terminated under an observation building, a brown half-octagon on stilts with windows that protruded, like the bridge of a fishing trawler. She recalled her first, swooning view of coyotes from the building. She hadn't been able to stop smiling, dizzy from the structure's sway in the gentle wind.

The pair of coyotes had beaten a wide, flat swath into the vegetation at the base of the fence, and she followed the trail. She was one-third of the way into the pen when the coyotes, without taking their eyes from her, loped toward the curve of the far end of the enclosure. They positioned themselves between her and the gate. Lynne continued walking, staring at her feet and musing. She balanced the pin stick on her shoulder, letting it bounce as her legs swung along the path. Covered in a mix of fallow alfalfa, grasses, and weeds, the Utah landscape was raw, feral.

The female coyote sniffed and pawed at the gate while the male hesitated diffidently behind his mate. Trotting toward the pen's edge, the female coyote stopped short of Lynne's footprints, as if the animal had hit the end of an invisible tether. The coyote swung her nose around; her body and tail followed it. She sniffed the ground, pawed at it, then squatted and urinated on a footprint.

Lynne, in the distance, eyes fixed on the ground in front of her, continued walking toward the middle of the pen. The coyotes trotted along the trail behind her, closing the distance. The male weaved along the path behind his advancing mate as if he were knitting a noose.

There was a growling, then—

Woof. Wuff.

Lynne heard two puffs, like breaths that escape when a person is punched in the stomach. She looked up, again present in time and place. Turning toward the sound, she saw the female coyote, only a few feet away, its head down, legs cocked as if ready to pounce.

People and predators don't live in simplified landscapes, even though human-impacted lands can appear pedestrian to the inured human eye. Our manicured sprawl is not so simple. It is actually a megalopolis of micro-habitats that create homes for rabbits, rats, mice, gophers, squirrels, and deer—thus spreading a tablecloth upon which mammalian predators can dine. Our ordinances and our affluence, combined with a longing for the greenness of idealized nature, create lushness between buildings. At a minimum, the greenways serve as sidewalks for coyotes, but they also provide them a peaceful, permanent home. Coyotes sleep undetected under shrubs in parks and backyards and know that city pickup trucks ambling by do not have varmint rifles at the ready, slung along rear windows.

Eric Gese, a researcher working for Wildlife Services, recounts observations of coyotes in Chicago: "We knew they were there because we had radio collars on them. It was incredible. All the people going by that had no idea."[24] The clever coyotes hid in plain sight, invisible to the thousands of people around them. "They'd wait until it was safe to cross the road. After the cars went by, they dashed across." (Another incarnation of the coyote: they're also ninjas.)

Given time and numbers, however, coyotes and their activities will not remain invisible. Researchers found that coyotes in Claremont, California, relied heavily on human pets as a food source in the winter and spring. Malibu's glitter may as well be the Serengeti for house cats, as their remains were found in 13.6 percent of coyote scats there.[25] One particularly clever pack of coyotes used a feral cat colony in Southern California first as a food source and then, after they had killed most of the cats, learned to satisfy themselves with cat food placed out for the felids by resident cat lovers. It may be a stretch to suggest, yet it is important not to underestimate the intelligence of carnivores: they may have reasoned that keeping one or two cats alive kept the food coming, like having a predictable egg a day instead of one final feast on the hen.

When coyotes and people occupy the same suburban corridors, an amplification of interaction is expected. Complaints of coyote attacks and predation on pets in suburban California reported to the US Department of Agriculture had increased from 17 to 281 incidents from 1991 to 2003. Over time, this works out to about a 30 percent increase per year, an exponential trajectory that dwarfs the stock market's best. The Vancouver Ministry of Environment, Lands, and Parks documented a 315 percent increase in coyote complaints during a ten year span ending in 1995. In Texas, reports of coyote attacks on pets rose more than four-fold for the decade ending in 2003.[26]

Given time, some coyotes will observe, learn and test the primates around them, especially young humans with the size, but not the speed, of a lamb. Between 1978 and 2003, there were eighty-nine coyote attacks on people in California. In seventy-seven of those reports, coyotes stalked children, chased individuals, or aggressively threatened adults. In about half of the reports, serious or fatal injury was thought likely if the child had not been rescued. Documented attacks occur not only within the historic range of the coyote in the southwest United States: a promising nineteen-year-old Canadian folk singer was killed by coyotes as she hiked on a popular Nova Scotia trail in late 2009.[27]

Up to this point, Lynne had very much enjoyed the predators she was studying. Now, however, two of her subjects were considering killing her.

The pen's exit was well over one hundred yards away. Blocking the path was a crouched and growling female coyote. Between the female and the gate was an enthusiastic male, dancing about like a drunken reveler waiting for the fireworks on Guy Fawkes Night. Lynne felt queasiness in her stomach and dryness in her mouth as she summoned the gumption to bark at them. She raised the pin stick and pointed it at the closest coyote, trying to appear intimidating: "Get away. Get away!"

The female coyote held her ground and stared at the pin stick, unimpressed. The male's excitement increased. He swooped behind the female, trying to position Lynne between himself and his mate. "I said go!" Lynne yelled. The coyotes dodged and darted, increasingly animated, as her voice quavered.

Lynne raised the stick again, still trying to be menacing, and the female darted toward it, biting and tearing at its padding. The more Lynne shouted, the quicker the animals paced and sniffed the air. Were they scoffing at the smell of fear? Lynne positioned her back against the fence. They couldn't get behind her, but she had to keep the stick up and pointed at the female, who continued to dart and bite at its edges. Lynne kept her eyes on the coyotes, afraid to look down. This slowed her progress over the uneven ground as she began to inch back toward the gate.

Lynne moved. The coyotes repositioned. The dance continued until she reached the exit. Extending the thin iron of the pin stick with her right hand, she felt for the latch with her left, slid the clasp up. Cracking the gate, she stepped out of the pen and closed the door, sliding the pin stick out at the last second. Fastening a carabineer, she was safe. The coyotes loped back into the interior of the pen and disappeared into the vegetation.

Lynne's hands began to shake. She dropped the pin stick, fell to her knees, and began to sob.

"They can get their own bloody crap out of that pen."

CHAPTER 2

PREDATORS, PEOPLE, AND PREY
Impacts and Interactions

In the big picture, Arion Vendergon was trying to determine how humans and predators could get along. At the moment, he was creeping along through a green pasture in northwestern Wisconsin on a run-down ATV. He careened and caromed around trees, using the agility of the vehicle as protection from aggressive, or perhaps just aggressively curious, mother cows. He pulled to a high spot, swung out the arms of an antenna and listened for each calf: a 100 pulse-per-minute signal indicated a calf was dead, 60 beeps per minute meant it was still alive. We listened. They were all alive that day.

I toured the pastures with Arion until we came to a weathered modular farmhouse. We stopped to chat with the farmer. Working in the West, especially on ranches the size of some eastern states, I expected to meet a tall, lanky man in cowboy garb, boots and hat. He would drop down out of his $60,000 truck, having recently left the comforts of his sprawling ranch-style home with a view. With a look of ostensible pensiveness, he'd stare toward the horizon, perhaps trying to make out the edge of his property's boundary. I'd expect that if he said anything at all, it would be about overbearing government and how the wolves, bears, coyotes, and mountain lions were yet another cog in the plot to destroy him, his family, and the entire western—that is American—way of life.

Wisconsin, however, is nothing like Texas or the American West, other than the obvious bond and love of the land that rural inhabitants share. The farmer stooped in front of us was a short, gray-haired grandmother who made me confront my own expectations almost as brutally as if she'd swatted my head with a broom. We chatted with her while overlooking the muddy lawn outside her thin-walled home. We'd already toured the entirety of her semi-wooded eighty acres. She smiled gracefully, and it was clear that she needed dental care, but she did not appear to be bothered. She was well past the age when most people retire, and her most pressing activity that day was moving a pile of debris with a vintage tractor. To the side of the house, there were burned boards and remnants of a conflagrated barn. Black soot and pitted lumber jutted from the mix of mud and packed grass like crosses in a decaying graveyard. She asked Arion if he was sure that he'd be able to find out if wolves took her calves. Arion smiled back charmingly. He had sparkling blue eyes, dark hair, and a broad-shouldered build that made him look like a 1960s leading man. His perfect white teeth twinkled.

Many calves go missing in wolf country, and Arion was trying to determine what proportion of missing animal cases could be attributed to death by wolf. A study in Idaho concluded that wolves in the West may kill eight cows for every one that is found, necropsied, and designated a victim of wolf predation.[1] Compensation schemes and estimates of economic impact lack teeth when cattle just disappear. To do an equivalent study in the eastern end of wolf range in the United States, Arion had lined up a few farms in Wisconsin and Minnesota and spent hundreds of hours bouncing along on his ATV to monitor the lives and deaths of calves.

I asked him about the surroundings, if it seemed that the farm was in disrepair to him, too. The farmer wasn't starving, surely, but she did seem to be letting things go, he explained, pointing back toward the mud and debris near her house.

Arion explained that she had been going through some hard times. Her husband died a few years ago, so she was trying to run the family business as a widow. Her sons and grandsons came over to help her when they could, but they had their own jobs and families. The economics were tough.

To monitor the livestock industry, the National Agricultural Statistics Service produces reports in more or less five-year cycles, with one report focusing on sheep and goats and another on cattle.

The cost of predation nationwide is high. Predators cost sheep and goat owners $20.5 million in 2010.[2] In the 2011 report on cattle, losses to predators totaled nearly 220,000 animals, costing $98.5 million.[3]

Depredations aren't the whole story, either, as some livestock producers' businesses are run so close to the margins that they calculate out losses not just in terms of cattle or sheep but in pounds per animal. Nearby predators—even if they don't kill—make cattle nervous. Cattle become more vigilant; they move more and eat less. Cattle exposed to predation, even when they are not injured, have been found to reduce the time they spend foraging from 88 percent to 44 percent of their day.[4]

The numbers of domestic animals that wolves kill, however, are miniscule when compared with the sheer volume of hamburger on the hoof in the United States. According to government tables in 2000, wolves did not even earn their own heading as a predator responsible for losses.[5] Coyotes, domestic dogs, cougars, bears, foxes, and even eagles and bobcats deserved rankings, but the wolf, for all of its controversy, was oddly absent. Its presence was still absent from sheep and goat loss reports in 2005.[6] By 2011, however, statistics for wolves killing cattle were included in government summaries, but their impact was minimal relative to other species.[7] Even vultures killed more cattle than wolves in 2010, accounting for 5.4 percent of losses compared with the wolves' 3.7 percent. Domestic dogs accounted for 9.9 percent, and cougars and bobcats together were 8.6 percent. Coyotes dominated, accounting for 53.1 percent of cattle kills. In fact, most livestock are raised nowhere near wolf range, and wolves don't have much access to beef. Where wolf populations are growing and overlapping with livestock, however, wolves can have a large effect, especially on a per capita scale. A wolf in Idaho is about ten times more likely to kill livestock than a coyote living in the same area.[8] Numbers are less certain in the midwestern wolf range, hence Arion's study.

I wondered how many of the 220,000 or so cows killed each year were the grandmother farmer's.

Just two. Two. It didn't sound like much.

Arion explained that she had a small herd and no margin for loss. She was a widow getting her cash from the sale of a few animals per year. The dead were cows with calves. The wolves ate her cash income for the whole year.

It's not the magnitude of the killing. It's the depth of the loss. It's how personal it feels.

No wonder some people hate these animals.

Few animals are as dichotomous as a wolf. The beast is an amalgamation of love, affection, hatred, and primordial fear. It is a symbol of power and of persecution, an organizer of the ideal, peaceful family unit, but a bloody demon of death when feeding. A hypostatic union of divine and animal. The stuff of myth and misinformation, and passion. People change their names to *Amaroq* to solidify a spiritual bond, adopting a Native American appellation for wolf.

The wolf spawns emotional rhetoric unheard of since the Civil War. To some, the wolf is a dull bludgeon of the Endangered Species Act, and to others, a sharp arrow aimed at states' rights. Case in point: Mike Jimenez, the wolf recovery coordinator in the northern Rocky Mountains, had collared and released wolves at a roadside in Wyoming. He was first charged with trespassing.[9] It was a way of being non-neighborly. Mike recounted to me that releasing the wolves on the side of the road brought him the additional charge of "littering." It was posturing, and the charges eventually went away, but the point is that the biological wolf cannot be separated from its symbolism.

Literally a woman who ran with wolves, Diane Boyd stood before a mix of wolf groupies, government biologists, and Wildlife Services employees. She preferred documenting the return of the wolf to the northern Rocky Mountains for the University of Montana's Wolf Ecology Project to addressing a crowded room, but there she was. The advocates listened attentively, hands clasped on their laps as if they were sitting in church. The Montana Wildlife Services specialists and district supervisors slouched, scowling, in the back of the room, cowboy hats on, arms folded across their chests.

It was April 20, 1999. Diane opened her presentation on wolf behavior at the 11th Annual Rocky Mountain Wolf Recovery Conference, at Chico Hot Springs Resort, in Pray, Montana: "It is in the literature and on the bumper stickers . . . 'Little Red Riding Hood lied!'" She had fairy-tale graphics on a slide.

The Wildlife Services employees smirked and rolled their eyes. Not this again. It wasn't long ago that Suzanne Stone, the Defenders of Wildlife point of contact for Rocky Mountain wolves, was dressed in a long red hood and cape and handing out literature with this very message. Suzanne was a primary sponsor and organizer of the meeting; she was listening attentively.

"We first hear that there has never been an attack on a human by a wolf in North America. Then a reliable report comes in, and we back-paddle," Diane said. "Should we be surprised if a wolf attacks someone?"

The Wildlife Services employees sat up a little. Others, who saw wolves as spiritual beings rather than flesh and blood animals, were restless. To them, scientists and technicians who interacted with the angelic animals were like saints seated at the right hand of the wolf. Diane was a high priestess. But her words were heresy.

It wasn't that Diane wasn't similarly passionate about wolves, but she remained an objective scientist. She did not succumb to the illusions and stereotypes created by distance and romantic dreams of the wolf's nature.

"So after that report we find some excuse and say that there has not been one documented report of a wolf harming someone in North America. Then someone is bitten in BC, and we say that there has never been a documented report of a wolf killing a human in North America. And we find out that the wolf could have had rabies, so it is 'There has never been a documented report of a healthy wolf killing a person in North America.'

"You know I'm not saying that there is a big threat, but we are painting ourselves into a corner. We are going to look pretty silly when we end up saying, 'There has never been a well-documented and proven incident of a healthy and non-habituated wolf that has killed an adult human on a Tuesday evening in the eastern half of North America.'" Her message seemed fresh and new. Perhaps it was lost on much of the crowd then. She wasn't trying to demonize wolves or to create a swell of fear, but she was trying to show that honesty and integrity would most help wolves in the long run.

It is true that until the 1990s there were no documented reports of healthy wolves killing people in the lower United States. Then again, there weren't any wolves there to kill anyone. Hunting wolves was ostensibly to protect livestock, but it had an intensity and degree of focus that suggested a higher calling. Persecution peaked between 1900 and 1950, the period in which most extirpations were completed. Afterwards, wolves were absent from all of the contiguous United States except for tiny remnants in remote parts of Minnesota and Michigan.[10]

Where both wolves and people share the landscape, wolves do indeed attack and kill humans. Wolves took 12 children in Holland in 1810 and 1811. The famous Beast of Gevaudan (which turned out to be two rather normal wolves) was said to have killed more than 64 people in south central France from 1764 to 1767. Wolves killed 136 people in Vimianzo, Spain, from 1957 to 1959. Wolves also took 60 children in the Bihar region of India from 1993 to 1995, and killed at least 22 children in Uttar Pradesh, India, in 1996.[11] The Alaska Department of Fish and Game confirmed that a thirty-two-year-old was killed by wolves in 2010.[12] By March of 2013, a wolf had made the first attack on a person in Manitoba, Canada.[13]

Looking back, I think the people that Diane Boyd was addressing should have reacted, but her message fell flat from the podium. She was far ahead of her time and perhaps they were confused by the paradoxical message. Wolves kill things and are certainly capable of killing people, but that is nothing to be ashamed of or defensive about.

Concluding that a wolf is either a bloodthirsty threat, or alternatively a beneficent spirit of the forest, is a dishonest dichotomy: red or white, both are unworthy of the complexity of the beast itself. Does denying the potential danger of a wolf deny the very form and presence of the wolf?

Yes.

Predators are designed to kill things. It is their job. The value of a wolf is its particular brand of wildness. Its value is precisely that it isn't, and shouldn't be expected to behave like, a human, a domestic dog, an angel, or a devil.

There are few things as unsavory as observing a wolf face-deep in a feeding orgy of steaming blood and guts while a suffering victim watches itself be disemboweled. This is the kind of attack a wolf will do enthusiastically. The human reaction, when faced with such an unpleasant acceptance of fact—a cognitive dissonance—is to create myth and symbol that extends beyond observation. Our stories about wolves mollify our disturbing emotions.

And emotion—indeed one in particular—is the root of the predator paradox. It is typically not one of the feelings worn on one's sleeve, like hatred or love. Those two feelings were expressed clearly in the different camps in Diane's audience. The actual underlying emotion that sustains the partisanship is rarely expressed or acknowledged, but it is the primary motivator for advocates and eradicators alike. It is the same emotion that Lynne Gilbert-Norton felt so vividly when a couple of bold coyotes cornered her. It is the whispered language between predator and prey. It is fear.

European settlers carried their psychological baggage about wolves with them across the Atlantic, elevating the myths and stories into the fabric of culture. But other mammalian predators impact us emotionally and physically, too. On August 15, 2013, a twelve-year-old girl was attacked by a bear near her home in Cadillac, Michigan. The media quickly connected the dots to a rash of six attacks across the country that week.[14]

A generalist species, black bears are not wholly dependent upon meat, like wolves or cougars are, and they usually prefer easy and stationary meals, such as crops, beehives, roots, and berries. The biggest black bears of eastern North America may approach eight hundred pounds in weight, but three hundred pounds is more likely for a male and two hundred for a female. They need lots of food and are certainly big enough to smack down a linebacker, but they are less bloodthirsty than they could be. Even a mother black bear with cubs is more likely to order the cubs up a tree and then run, rather than attack an intruder. Stephen Herrero's famous book on the subject, *Bear Attacks: Their Causes and Avoidance*, documents five hundred injuries to humans resulting from encounters with black bears.[15] For such a powerful animal, it is fortunate that 90 percent of injuries they cause don't even begin to approach lethality. Such injuries are usually limited to small bites, scratches, and bruises. From 1900 to 1980, twenty-three fatalities were recorded. The American black bear is to the genus *Ursus* what the coyote is to *Canis*. They are more likely to live much more closely with us than are their much more powerful big brothers—the brown, or grizzly bear, *Ursus arctos*.

Brown bears are distributed widely across North America and Eurasia, but in the populated areas of the contiguous United States the subspecies grizzly bear gets the most press. Large males may approach a thousand pounds in weight. It is sometimes difficult to believe that in the early 1800s, perhaps 50,000 grizzly bears wandered between the Pacific coast and the Great Plains. By 1975, only a handful remained in six populations. Now, with only 1,200–1,400 wild grizzly bears in existence, they are no longer the lords of the landscape they used to be, but where they do exist they are key players, killing about 650 sheep and injuring about 50 people between 1992 and 2004. Herrero documented 165 injuries to humans resulting from encounters with brown bears in North America from 1900 to 1980, including 19 deaths.[16]

In the numbers game, however, and due to its very small range in the western United States, the grizzly is unlikely to be encountered by most cows, sheep, or suburbanites, and probabilities of damage to more than local livestock are low. You won't see a grizzly in Yosemite. Even tourists in Yellowstone are unlikely to see them. The animals aren't really secretive or shy, just rare and dispersed.

There seems to be a comfortable belief that the edge between human and wildlife is distinct. As a result, when interactions occur, the impact is heightened. Hence the amplification of surprise and grief in the tragedy when a young boy is lost to a marauding bear on Salt Lake City's doorstep. The spot where eleven-year-old Samuel Ives was pulled from his tent by a black bear was not wilderness, but within sight of a sprawling urban corridor of three million people.

As of the fall of 2013, the issue of culpability for the boy's death remained a focus of legal wrangling. The case against the state was initially dismissed due to the legal interpretation that the state is not responsible for natural conditions on the land. If someone falls off a cliff, for instance, the state can't be sued because it cannot be held responsible for that natural danger. Upon appeal, however, the Utah Supreme Court ruled that bears are "not natural conditions on the land," as the lower court had ruled.[17]

The state Division of Wildlife Resources had classified the animal as a Level III, nuisance bear—and slated it for termination—because it had threatened campers the night before. But the spot where the Ives stayed was not an official, developed campground. No warning was transmitted. Subsequently, on Father's Day 2007, a young boy died yards from his dad. The family successfully sued the Forest Service, but was it the fault of the federal government? The bear? The state? The family?

Who was going to prevent such a tragedy from occurring again? How would it be done?

About 138 people are killed by lightning each year in the United States.[18] With 41 deaths from cougars documented between 1890 and 2004, that makes a person almost four hundred times more likely to be struck by lightning than to be killed by a cougar. But which fate provokes the most fear? One death by the secretive stalker in Colorado can create a best seller.[19] Mountain lions are subject to the same contradictory emotions we seem to have regarding all of our predators: we fear them, yet love them as well. Devotion to the predator led to passage of California's Proposition 117 in 1990. At that time, despite a healthy estimated population of four thousand to six thousand, mountain lions became a "specially protected species."[20] Thus, with a vote, the public became the authority that managed mountain lions, leaving trained biologists wondering why they bothered to go to graduate school. Based on scientific and expert opinion, the species showed no sign of endangerment in the state, yet the proposition passed easily. Mountain lion hunting is now illegal in California, as is the taking, injuring, possessing, transporting, importing, or selling any mountain lion or part of a mountain lion. Perhaps fourteen lions per year are removed for public safety reasons, including some that are removed to protect a species that actually is in danger: bighorn sheep of the Sierra Nevada.

Mountain lion, puma, or cougar are just regional variations in names of the same species, *Puma concolor*. Limited mostly to the western United States, these predators are quiet, invisible death machines. Killing almost thirteen thousand head of livestock and causing about a million dollars in damage per year, lions are a very distant third behind coyotes and domestic dogs, with only 5.7 percent of sheep and goat losses to predators, for example, attributable to the big cats.[21]

Expect numbers to rise as the species expands its haunts.[22] Current cougar range covers a swath of the western United States, from the coast to the middle of Montana and angling southeast into the lower sections of Texas. But verified cougar sightings outside of their range from 1990 to 2010 place a smattering of reports throughout the Midwest, into Wisconsin, Illinois, and down through Missouri, Arkansas, and Louisiana, and as far east as Indiana. They are dipping down into Maine and upper New York and expanding up the Florida peninsula from the little subspecies population locally known as the Florida panther.

David Baron cataloged the statistics as an NPR reporter and made a living touring the country telling people about it. His book, *The Beast in the Garden*, was largely about the death of Scott Lancaster in Idaho Springs, Colorado. Baron's work details, with sprinklings of intriguing symbolism and hyperbole, the gruesome aspects of what was done to the young man's body. Within the first few pages Baron compares the corpse to a victim of ritualized murder, juxtaposing the predation with commentary on the Aztecs, who "hauled prisoners up high pyramids and cut out their beating hearts as an offering to the sun." Baron also writes that Scott Lancaster's murderer hollowed out his body "like a pumpkin" and scattered vegetation over him, "as if to signify something profound."[23]

Baron's description of the scene—as if it was the work of a depraved serial killer—pissed off Wendy Keefover-Ring, who at the

time was with an organization called Sinapu. The group was hell-
bent on advocating for predators in the western United States. She
attacked Baron, stating that "the book's sloppy methodology, un-
satisfying leaps in logic, historical inventions" and attributions of
"human characteristics to wildlife," along with "unsound ethical
reasoning" were a classic case of fear mongering and profiteering.[24]
The claws were out and there was a lot of snarling between the
lines, in defense of cougars.

"Baron's pumas-as-Aztec-priests or knife-wielding-surgeons
makes interesting reading and taps into people's primal fears
about large predators. Apparently this tactic has worked since he
has achieved enough interest to generate a second printing of his
book . . ." It wasn't the lion's fault, she argued, nor was the "hippie-
bred, herbal-tea-drinking, animal-venerating, nature-loving culture" of Boulder, Colorado, to blame.[25] Her crosshairs were aimed
directly at the messenger.

Ultimately, Keefover-Ring worried that *The Beast in the Garden*
exhibited unforgivable anachronistic thinking and was an attempt
to return "us to the turn of the nineteenth century, the time when
the dominant American culture—conservationists included—believed that predators were evil and ravenous and we humans (as
well as the deer) were innocent victims." In her view, if a cat kills a
man and the press sensationalizes it, people will unanimously turn
against predators and seek to ruthlessly rid them from the West
again. She had a point. The pendulum can swing both ways.

Reading the vituperative point-counterpoint in the fall 2005 issue of *Environmental Law* is like reading the parable of the blind
men and the elephant. One blind man feels a leg and declares the
elephant is just like a tree. Another caresses the trunk and is certain
that an elephant is a type of snake. Keefover-Ring argued about
cougars, and Baron made assertions about people, but they were at
opposite ends of an even more complex animal.

On January 12, 1995, eight hefty aluminum crates, looking like ar-
mored dog kennels, passed into the north entrance of Yellowstone
National Park. A caravan of patrol cars ensured that the wolves and
federal dignitaries that accompanied them would all arrive at a hid-

den pen in Lamar Valley, a good forty miles into the park. Far from their homes of capture in Alberta, the wolves were scheduled for what is known as a "soft-release," in the patois of wildlife biologists.

The constraints of the pens forced the wolves to become accustomed to the sights, sounds, and smells of the area. They would be taught that what they saw beyond the galvanized fabric of the fence was their home. After ten weeks, the gates opened; in an instant, wolves resumed their status as top dog in Yellowstone. It was a boast that couldn't be made since the last pair was trapped out of Lamar in 1926.[26] Wolf populations were recovering, with support. Things had changed, but were we ready?

During the 1990s, the wolf population of the northern Rocky Mountains began rebounding as numbers increased exponentially. In 1980, just a scattering of wolves lived in northwest Montana; by 1985 the count was 13. Five years later, however, that number more than doubled, then doubled again—to 66—in 1995, when reintroductions to Yellowstone and Idaho occurred. The subsequent population growth was astounding. Suddenly, there were at least 101 wolves roaming Montana, Wyoming, and Idaho. By 2000, the population had quadrupled, to at least 437; by 2005 it was 1,016. Most recently, counts indicate that 1,674 wolves live in the northern Rockies.[27]

Wolves are not unlike coyotes in their potential for exponential population growth. There are currently about seventy thousand gray wolves in North America, occupying about half of their historic range. Ironically, this poster child of charismatic predators and lightning rod for controversy is no dusky seaside sparrow about to blink out of existence. Wolves are here in force, and their presence ripples not only through the human landscape, but through broader ecological systems as well.

Wolf expansion in the western United States is more than a spiritual rebirth or a success of the Endangered Species Act. It is also a great experiment on the landscape of Idaho, Montana, and Wyoming, measured not only by the number of wolves, but by the number of aspen.

The significance of returning an ecosystem's top predator became apparent in the years following wolf reintroduction. Bill Ripple and his colleagues at Oregon State University were the first to put the pieces together. Ripple boldly announced that the presence of wolves corresponded with dramatic change in the vegetative landscape. Wolves, like ecological keystones supporting the ecosystem, affected entire species and habitats.[28]

The story starts in the wetlands of Yellowstone. Since the early part of the century, when wolves were actively removed from Yellowstone, vegetation in the park's northern range had been struggling. Aspens, willows, and cottonwoods were not regenerating. The plants simply could not grow from tender sprout to invincible tree before being grazed to death. The culprits, scientists concluded, were elk. Post–wolf reintroduction research suggested that aspen were growing better and higher in the riparian areas that were encircled by wolf territories. Wolves could not eat every elk in Yellowstone, but the threat of predation they posed could change prey behavior. Naïve elk were dead quickly. Fear is the engine of wariness and survival for all prey species.[29] Elk most certainly could gauge the new danger after seeing a few of their calves torn to bloody pieces and consumed. Feeling the fear, elk began to avoid wolves and the open wetlands where they would be most vulnerable. Aspen and cottonwoods enjoyed the respite.

Thus, wolves created an ecology of fear that rippled through the food web. Elk remained in the park because it was their home and source of sustenance, but because of the fear of predation, they altered their travel and feeding habits. No longer would they linger on the edges of creeks, lazily slurping up saplings. The aspen and cottonwoods could pursue their own prerogative to dominate the landscape. The impact was greater than the obvious—evidence supported the hypothesis that the top dog wasn't just a guard dog but also an unlikely farmer.

Apex predators will eat their way down into the food web and each strand, connected one to another, will pluck others throughout the ecosystem. This top-to-bottom disruption of species abundance and composition is termed a *trophic cascade* by ecologists and has become a popular narrative for science writers.[30] It is a fascinating tale, as one charismatic species demonstrates its crucial ecological importance. Wolves are not unique in this role, however, but are only some of the most recent predators observed to produce the top-down effect.

Coyotes on the landscape indirectly protect waterfowl and other species. Raccoons and foxes are efficient nest predators, but when coyotes are present the smaller predators' populations suffer—to the benefit of ground- and shrub-nesting birds.[31]

The other predators have fascinating indirect effects on ecosystems too. Cougars kill deer, but they simultaneously act as doctors to populations in what is hypothesized as the *sanitation effect*. For example, chronic wasting disease has swept over deer populations in Colorado, concerning wildlife managers and hunters alike. The disease, like the horrific mad cow disease, transforms deer in their prime into emaciated skeletons of their former selves.

A little wrongly-folded protein, called a prion, is the culprit. The particle works like Vonnegut's Ice Nine, but within an animal's brain. The native state protein, correctly folded, goes about assisting cells, but when touched by a prion, its conformation changes into an insoluble particle that aggregates with other such particles to form plaques. Spongiform encephalopathy results, and brain tissue, instead of being solid and healthy, looks like a slice of sponge on a microscopic slide.

Humans can't tell the difference between an infected deer and a non-infected one before late-stage, horrible symptoms are manifested, but cougars can. In the Front Range of Colorado, cougars actually select for infected deer, slowing the spread of the disease through the population.[32] The particular prion appears to be unique to deer, so cougars may feast with little worry of contracting the disease. Thus predators do more than kill; they prune, helping to clean and maintain the health of prey populations.

The top dog, be it aquatic or terrestrial, is a prime mover in a web of connections. But which top consumers do we want driving the system, humans or the others? Why do we choose one over the other?

The return of wolves, cougars, bears, and even lowly coyotes heralds the return of an aspect of nature nearly forgotten in developed countries. Predation has again become a cause of human death. The probability is miniscule, but the threat is growing, and I can't argue for anything but a zero tolerance policy against predation on humans. It is a challenge of the paradox: to have dangerous predators on the landscape but not to suffer any risk from their presence (unless, of course, one desires that thrill).

For students and wildlife biologists, working with North American predators is a lesson in grasping contradictions. It involves balancing love and hate with fear. The coyote is beautiful but also scrappy and raw. It is a symbol of the West, a bringer of fire in Native American legend. An apotheosis but also a trickster, a scoundrel, a killer of helpless lambs. A varmint. Mark Twain insults the coyote in *Roughing It:* "The meanest creatures despise him and even the flea would desert him for a velocipede."[33] Such schizophrenia in assigning personalities isn't limited to our view of the coyote. All of our North American carnivores have complex identities. Sometimes wolves are the great Native American Brother. Other times they are the devil incarnate, chasers of calves and little hooded girls, consumers of grandmothers. Bears, especially mother next to curious cub, are terrifying, but they are also personified as gentle, caring Teddy and Smokey. What are these creatures really, and why do they impact our myths and morals so? Why is our relationship with them so difficult to pin down?

We can turn to scientists for answers, but researchers are hardly of a unified mind, having quite a varied history themselves. The field biologists of today were finishing school at the tail end of the '70s environmental revolution. The world was changing, and the discipline was developing along with it. Newcomers challenged the uniformity of wildlife management's hook-and-bullet establishment.

The newbies devoured the knowledge of wildlife biology, but they had different motivations than those who had entered the field in previous decades. They were just as interested in the animals, but grew queasy at the thought of shooting them. They were satisfied just to know the beasts and to categorize the obscure habits of a forest primate or a snake. For them, it was a gleeful experience solely to catch a glimpse of the face, or the ass for that matter, of a bear. For these students, the animal experience was more about communion than consumption. Good-old-boy wildlife management struggled with what felt like a hostile takeover by art history majors; the new students marveled at the wonders of wildlife the way others swooned over the *Mona Lisa*. Art was for art's sake, not a gift to spoil. Shooting a wolf, in this up-and-coming mindset, was like murdering Da Vinci. This schizophrenia, already ensconced in public attitudes, became part of the profession too.

In my own memories of growing up in the '80s, even before I had the notion of becoming a wildlife biologist, a few images and issues stand out. I recall the great ad campaign showing a scrap of litter blowing across the American West, seen by a lone Native American who shed a single tear, lamenting the devastation. There was the great post–*Silent Spring* furor over DDT. I remember images of broken bald eagle eggs, the shells too thin to support life. I remember feeling the guilt before I had the opportunity to earn it: We'd trashed our environment, poisoned our water, and killed off our own national symbol. We'd paved over paradise, and the only eagles I heard were on the radio.

A narrow memory, perhaps, but the influx of environmentalism into wildlife management happened for good reasons. Non-game and predatory animals were on the verge of extirpation in the United States. Simultaneously, we were realizing that the earth's resources weren't unlimited, and that our actions were leading to the annihilation of many animals that we had come to value—ironically due to their human-caused rarity. The sentiment was no longer fringe: Richard Nixon banned poisons on public lands and signed some of the most progressive environmental protection legislation.

At a time when Americans are more concerned than ever with conserving our natural resources . . . nothing is more priceless and more worthy of preservation than the rich array of animal life with which our country has been blessed.
—Richard Nixon, statement on signing the
  Endangered Species Act of 1973[34]

❧ ❧ ❧

We were discovering phenomena such as trophic cascades and the fact that top predators were essential components of ecosystems. We wanted predators back. Nixon kicked the pendulum and reversed its direction. We set about restoring the populations of the very predators we had persecuted so vehemently for many years.

This is where the current story begins, where the depths of the ambivalence manifest. With great enthusiasm and expense, predators, such as wolves, were reintroduced to their former homes, then promptly shot. Yellowstone National Park biologists collared the charismatic "rock star" she-wolf 832F, yet the animal later died—legally hunted—after stepping beyond the confines of the park. The irony sparked international outrage, but no change in policy.[35] The great campaign against wildlife continues, with both people and nonpartisan species dying as collateral damage. Great industries of advocacy rise up and litigate against the dysfunction. Conservation groups disseminate propaganda asserting that the very survival of wolves is at stake,[36] when in reality, wolves are spread across the whole northern hemisphere, with more than seventy thousand in North America alone. The US Fish and Wildlife Service tries to delist the gray wolf throughout the United States, then awaits litigation.[37] There isn't much room for biology in the arguments.

Senators—sick of the never-ending push/pull of delisting, litigation, and relisting—rebelled. Anger and resentment about federal intervention on western lands was nearly as heated as the posturing that led to Manassas. The wolf became a tool of brinkmanship in arguments over the federal budget. It took a literal act of Congress, but in 2011 wolf management in Montana and Idaho became exempt from the Endangered Species Act. A Democrat from Montana, Senator Jon Tester, and a Republican from Idaho, Mike Simpson, attached a bold rider to budget legislation and, with a signature, *Canis lupus* was delisted in much of the northern Rockies.[38]

The cause of the political and scientific disconnect, ultimately, is the predator paradox. These gorgeous varmints have a complicated impact on our collective psyche and pocketbook. Citizens and scientists collectively want a safe environment with a cheap and abundant food supply yet demand that dangerous carnivores expand across our landscape free from the risk of extinction. Simply, it's the human proclivity of "wanting to have one's cake and eat it too."

How can we overcome the predator paradox? How do we address its complexities in the suburban landscape, domestic pasture, or the recreational mountain cabin? What about the different hopes, dreams, values, and fears of the people and predators that inhabit these places? How can we balance it all?

We will find some answers by embracing both the nature of diversity and the diversity of nature.

CHAPTER 3

FOOD

An Inseparable Connection

Lynne navigated the grocery cart, referring to it as a "trolley," through the cavernous market aisles. Canned beans topped her list. She gasped when she reached the bean aisle, paralyzed by the superfluity before her.

"We'd have one brand back home," she said, not knowing which can to choose.

It wasn't long ago that receiving an orange at Christmas was magical. Today, by leaving trails of fossil fuel emissions across the sky and oceans, we can have an orange, tangerine, nectarine, banana, or any sort of tomato at any time of year in nearly any town or remote highway pit stop in North America. Not only that, but one can usually choose between the organic or inorganic variety and then several different brands of each. And it is the same with our meat, poultry, and dairy. We grow fat and feel entitled because the simplest things come too easy. There is the *how* of so much agricultural capacity, but for now we will consider the equally important *why*.

Insatiable, we don't want just to have our cake and eat it too. We want seconds, thirds, and infinite variety. We are absolutely and fully dependent on the environment that grows our food and impacts our wildlife populations, but mostly oblivious to the connection.[1]

Blind to the process, we push our farms to extremes.[2] We banished pests and carnivorous threats. We've changed the courses of mighty rivers, created wondrous ways of fertilizing and weeding great monocultures, crossbred crops until we've toughened their skins for international transport, and magnified hedonics to best match the human palate. We've pried into the genetic codes of plants and animals and learned to clone and create in new ways. With 550 million Big Macs sold per year in the United States (seventeen per second), it is clear that we like our food big, fat, and cheap.[3] When predators kill our livestock and damage our crops, they complicate matters and increase prices. Estimates indicate that cattle and calf losses from predators reached 220,000 head during 2010, for a loss of $98.5 million.[4] That is a lot of ninety-nine-cent hamburgers.

Food production alters environments, and altered environments impact predators. The central question: Do we want to have predators around, or do we want to keep the price of burgers low and have a choice of hundreds of types of beans in small-town grocery marts? Or is there some balance?

"I chose to be a vegetarian in my youth," Lynne said. She grew up in England, a little island really, that is almost completely tamed and devoid of any remnants of the large beasts that once hunted its greenways. England became a safe place where the locals harnessed resources, removed threats, and catapulted their capabilities into wealth and world dominance. It is a history we ought to consider as we continue to develop the American West.

Three lions appear on England's coat of arms, symbolizing great power for a land the magnificent beasts don't inhabit. In an echo of the same irony in the New World, the grizzly was extirpated from California within decades of the gold rush, but remains a shameless symbol on that state's flag. As powerful as the animals are as symbols, the living creatures receive a different type of respect.

In Hyrum, Utah, there is sometimes a stench from thousands of nervous cattle being held briefly before their final trip to the abattoir. If you lived there, you would have grown accustomed to the odor and inured to the pungent redolence of death. Hardly anyone on the south end of Cache Valley thinks about the mechanized, modernized, industrialized slaughter that churns out butchered bodies continuously. If you notice at all, you recognize it as the smell of money and go about your business.

It's a simple economic event to line up beef like parts in a disassembly line—for that is what it is—and move the beasts through as if they were nuts, bolts, doors, wheels, and windshields. The modern food infrastructure is a miracle, and perhaps we should be proud of our accomplishments. We can grow more food in the United States than we are able to eat and export. We even grow corn to feed our cars ethanol while others in the world are starving.

Rosamond Naylor and colleagues at the Center for Environmental Science and Policy at Stanford University reported in the journal *Science* that mechanized food—defined as food produced through large-scale, intensive operations with confined animals— accounts for about 75 percent of the world's chickens, two-thirds of eggs, and almost half of the world's pork. "Livestock remains the world's largest user of land, but its use has shifted steadily from grazing to the consumption of feed crops."[5]

The authors summarize the problem as one of disconnect. The costs to the environment and resource base are separated in time and space not only from the industrial livestock systems but also from the consumer base. The language is disturbing: we acquire our food, which was once a living, perhaps sentient being, from a *system*. Intimacy with the environment is fading away, replaced by distribution from a conglomerate that controls every link in the chain, from feed to animal to meat to big-box store. And as the price of feed goes down and the wealth of nations goes up, the demand and production of meat grows exponentially. The chasm between human and nature widens and deepens.

We've pushed efficiency to the extreme. The average time needed to produce a broiler chicken in the United States plummeted from seventy-two days in 1960 to forty-eight days in 1995; simultaneously, slaughter weight rose from 1.8 kg. to 2.2 kg. The focus of growth in the agricultural industry is the monogastric animal: chickens and hogs, which can convert complicated feeds into protein quickly. Furthermore, the relatively short lifespan and rapid reproduction of a chicken allows for high-speed genetic modification. Expect less beef in your diet in the future: "Annual growth in hog and poultry production in developing countries was twice the world average in the 1990s."[6] Cattle are a more environmentally sustainable alternative than other sources of industrialized meat because they can magically turn nonirrigated grass and low-quality feed that humans can't digest into useable protein, whereas chickens and hogs require legumes and cereals that compete with other human-edible crops for water and space.

As they sprawl, reproduce, and eat, humans will always have an impact on the environment, but are we tempering those impacts? Are we acting with some cognizance of the other species around us, or just single-mindedly taming the land? Growing legumes and grains, especially in climates that can't naturally support them, destroys native grasslands by converting the land into artificial monoculture. The impacts are multiplied when great rivers are dammed, and when tunnels, ditches, and great over-mountain pumps are installed. We then feed the largesse to pigs, converting already edible foodstuffs into pork.

Industrial livestock operations require huge amounts of water, much of it pumped into feed production. But such operations affect water quality, as confined animals excrete concentrated nutrients, pathogens, antibiotics, and other chemicals back into groundwater.

A more alluring and sustainable food production system would rely on cattle or bison roaming free in grass-fed harmony with the environment. The catch: unprotected, slowly growing, hooved protein is susceptible to marauding predators. Even now, NASS lists of conflicts with mammalian predators focus entirely on predation on livestock. The link between most people and predators is their food. To have both predators and an inexpensive and abundant food supply, we need to identify economically feasible ways to work with and within natural systems rather than divorced from them.

Just as North Americans rely on their farmers and ranchers, students like Lynne rely on the Predator Research Facility's staff to do required animal husbandry. For Lynne, this creates the potential for clashes between Old and New Worlds, but diversity is also the stuff of tolerance, understanding, and inspiration.

Patrick Darrow, an animal-care technician at the Predator Research Facility, had greater ambitions than throwing moist, raw slop of slaughterhouse by-products to coyotes and watching them lap it up greedily. Raised on a farm in southern Idaho, Patrick chuckled at the irony of his current job caring for coyotes. "I like coyotes as far as that goes, but if I was on the farm and saw one across the field, I'd shoot at it," he said. "Maybe if I was alone I wouldn't," he admitted, "but if my brother was there, I'd *have* to."

When pressed, he said, "It's a farm. That's what's expected. I mean, it isn't like they cause us any grief or anything. We just raised a few cattle and the coyotes don't bother them much. It's just what you do. It's probably a combination of growing up on a farm in a small town, and religion, too." The ethics of Patrick's Mormon upbringing were similar to those held by many Americans. Nature was something God gave mankind to use, to take advantage of. In his young mindset, if we took care of ourselves, "nature would take care of itself."

He smiled, adding, "And anyway, about us shooting at coyotes —it wasn't a big deal. It wasn't like we ever hit anything."

Patrick served his missionary obligation to the Church of Jesus Christ of Latter-day Saints in Georgia. Upon returning, he resumed his studies in wildlife from Utah State University and sought a wife and a job. He turned away from the family farm. He admitted that working as an animal-care technician for the federal government allowed him to separate home from work, a luxury of disconnection and rest that farmers don't have. For them, work and home are one and the same.

With farming, there is always uncertainty. Weather, pests— anything—could destroy the crops. It is like gambling for a living, except you can never, ever, step away from the table. Whether or not you get paid depends on some buyer in China or on Budweiser's margin. Farmers irrigate the crops with their sweat; they sustain the meat with their own hearts and lungs. They know where food comes from and the hardships intrinsic to its production.

"So why did you break away from your family farm?" I asked, expecting a tirade about the long, irregular hours or toil.

"Hay fever." He smiled. "I like working with animals and that aspect, but really the hay fever kills me. So that's why I wanted to be a biologist." It wasn't in him to completely break away from nature and go into law enforcement like his brother, so wildlife biology was a good compromise. The profession still had the animals and regular contact with the natural world, but it also supplied a regular paycheck and freedom from overwhelming allergens.

His farming background gave Patrick a much different perspective from that of some of the researchers at the facility, especially Lynne. Patrick had hunted coyotes before, using a call and camouflage to bring them in close enough for a shot. It wasn't a long-term passion in him, but an objective and even intellectual challenge to overcome: how to outsmart a coyote on its own turf. He had to be careful, however, how much he discussed such activities with his colleagues. "I really like Lynne," he said, "but there are some topics that I just don't bring up." Lynne had to physically leave the site if animals, especially ones she had worked with, needed to be euthanized.

Where Patrick enjoyed the omelet, Lynne seemed more focused on not breaking any eggs. The two were representative of the varying approaches that one species, *Homo sapiens*, takes to a fundamental process. Everyone eats, and how they connect with food is how they connect with the environment, which in turn is how they connect with mammalian predators.

I bite into a burger, but the flavor is more than that of lean meat and condiments. It is spiritual and timeless.

It is the taste of a past morning at a time of year when the sun is reluctant to rise. The rays are cold and low on the horizon. My legs and lungs ache as I posthole through the deep snow, trying to get to the top of the ridge before it is too late. I see the animals on the next ridge.

My heart pounds. I am nervous and extremely uncomfortable. My first thought is to panic, to turn and run and not complete the mission. I woke early and trudged a thousand feet up a mountain already, but when the decision becomes tangible my knees weaken. I fill with self-doubt and question my ability to shoot straight. I fear making a poor shot, causing unnecessary pain for my prey and the ignominy of hypocrisy for myself.

I am hungry and tired, but the pain and worry feel correct. I should feel the connection. Back when I applied for an elk permit, I told myself it was better to harvest my own grass-fed, predator-friendly, organic, hormone-free, humanely slaughtered meat. It was better to connect with and know the source of my food. I want to join the natural system, rather than continue fighting with it.

Dropping my pack and slinging the rifle, I begin the stalk, moving low, staying in cover and downwind of the small herd. I crawl to the edge of the forest and steady the rifle against the tree that obscures me from view. I breathe slowly, completing my internal conversation with death. The life lost will not be my own, but I want it to be as quick, painless, and sudden as I would want for myself. I contain my thoughts and focus. On a gentle exhalation I adduct my finger against the trigger—a slow, even draw, as though I am beckoning a lover toward me.

How much less meat would each of us eat if we had to harvest our own? How much more would we respect nature if we lived with it, versus storing its ideals away in parks and on nature shows? What would happen if those of us who sprawl across the landscape learned to bond with it, to cut a few links in the chain that binds us to an agricultural industry that demands our bloated consumption?

To this day, when I pull a package of elk meat from the freezer, my heartbeat quickens. I relive the moment of taking a life in order to sustain my own. I remember the animal suddenly disappearing from view, a sentient, feeling animal removed forever from existence.

I see the other animals look around. They heard the shot, like distant thunder. They do not run in panic. Unaware of my presence, they stare dumbly in various directions. They do not seem to notice that one of their herd has collapsed in a heap. After a few moments, they wander over the hill and out of sight. I stumble down to her.

"Thank you," I say when I arrive at the carcass. It is the only prayer I know anymore. "Thank you." I lay my hand on the lifeless elk and ready my knife.

I remember the pain and exhaustion of the next few hours just as vividly. Elk are always on a steep slope. It takes hours to gut and bag the elk and prepare her for the trip off of the mountain. I use cords to hold her legs in place, but when one hoof is out of the way, the other drops or slides. I slip in the snow and fall. Opening the chest cavity, I see that her liver is gone, jellified by the shockwave of the bullet. This animal died instantaneously and unexpectedly, the way I hope I eventually will. "Thank you," I say again, this time with more relief than reverence. I return to work.

Many more hours of struggle remain. I must haul her miles off the mountain. I must cut the steaks and roasts and grind the burger and sausages. There is pain and suffering, and for me that is the point. The connection has been stolen from us by the inventors of Styrofoam and plastic wrap. We have forgotten that nature should hurt a little.

People remember the sweat and toil when they grow and kill much of what they eat. I sometimes wonder why more don't do it, but I know several reasons why it took me so long before I found my natural connection to food and nature. Owning a gun is scary for someone who did not grow up around them. Hunting seems so foreign and intimidating, especially given a popular image of bloodthirsty bubbas stinking of cheap beer and ATV fumes. There are many philosophical reasons why people refuse to hunt, too.

Lynne acknowledges that she could never kill anything herself, and asserts that her feelings on the matter are justified and can't be dismissed.

I am comfortable with her reasoning. She is right.

Patrick would argue that everyone in New York and Boston can't be expected to go out into the woods and hunt either. It is more efficient to specialize, to have some folks farm and ranch.

And that is okay too.

The connection to wildness and predation can be spiritual. It can be logical, and it can serve economic purposes. It certainly does not require that all of us don loin cloths and live in hollowed-out stumps in the woods. But if no one accepts even a modicum of pain or any of the realities of suffering and death, we are dead in the water. If we are to learn to live with predators, we have to relearn how to interact with nature. Those of us with predatory instincts must be able to express those behaviors, too—bonding in our own way with the other predators. For good reasons that we shall see, each of us must still learn to interact with nature, but we have to do it on our own, individual terms.

It would help if people knew more about where their food comes from. It could help if they ate less meat. I wish we would all buy local and accept the extra costs and leanness of grass-fed beef or buffalo. Some proportion of us could dive spiritually deep and obtain our protein while eschewing farmed animals completely—harvesting it ourselves in the form of deer or elk. There is no environmentally better choice for needed protein than wild game, when hunting is properly regulated by state agencies. Grass-fed, hormone-free, free-range—the list of benefits goes on.

Resolving the predator paradox cannot be accomplished through a single, self-righteous choice of action. It requires embracing quite the opposite. The question is not whether Little Red Riding Hood was wrong or right: she was both. This is not to trivialize the issue as a question of moral relativism, right and wrong watered down to meaningless gray. There are absolutes and truths: A dead wolf cannot kill a cow—that is an absolute truth. But there are other ways to keep a wolf from killing a cow and reasons for choosing one method over another. If we don't exclude predators by planting monocultures that turn into feedlot fodder, or kill predators to protect the calves, we are tolerating them in our food production system.

Eating less industrialized meat can mean fewer domestic hooves on the ground, which lessens our impact on the environment. This approach can in turn reduce conflicts between humans and predators. Purchasing from small, predator-friendly farms is another way to strike a balance, as is harvesting your own meat. Hunting has an added value aspect, since it reestablishes the link between predator and prey within us. It can remind us that humans, bears, wolves, cougars, and coyotes are too closely connected to live well without each other. Hunting closes the gap we created with the first shrink-wrapped supermarket tenderloin. Killing and carrying an animal links the emotions of fear, pain, and loss to the meat. It reveals the real cost of consumption. In my own sense of morality, there is nothing inherently wrong with experiencing the pleasure of turning one animal's calories into my own, but in my view the animal should not suffer alone.

CHAPTER 4

PERCEPTIONS THAT FUEL THE PARADOX

Peggy Callahan had about twenty dogs in her kitchen. Most were German shepherds, or at least mostly Alsatian, but in the moil the exact number and breed composition were impossible to determine. It was all fur and panting. Nearly two dozen tongues lolled and dripped. The sea of black and tan expanded and contracted. Ripples of yips and barks ebbed, flowed, and swelled, often initiated by an inadvertent toe stomping as animals jockeyed for prime position in the kitchen. Other times, the pandemonium began for no apparent reason. Maybe there was a subtle bump perceived as a hip slam and the pressure was enough to spark a conflagration of barking.

It takes all kinds, I thought. *Everyone has a different approach to life.*

I waited for Peggy to finish collecting the breakfast dishes while my own dog, a calm, refined German shepherd named Gretchen, cowered and leaned against my legs. Trained for search and rescue, among other things (Peggy called her "Gretchen the Wonder Dog"), my dog was not enjoying the visit as much as I was. She was an intellectual, much more comfortable around people than other dogs.

A small visitor appeared quietly at the other end of the living room, initiating a new wave of excited barks and canine collisions. Peggy's four-year-old daughter, Megan, had emerged from her room, rubbing her eyes sleepily and clutching a ragged stuffed animal. Waifish, her disheveled blonde locks cascaded onto the loosely fitting frock that served as her nightgown. She stepped softly into the kitchen, looking as though she had come from a *Les Miserables* poster.

"Get out of the way. Go." Arms outstretched, the child waded through like a tiny Moses. The dogs parted just enough to allow her passage. She climbed onto the barstool next to me, and I expected her to pour herself a cup of coffee or maybe to order a morning shot of scotch. She grabbed a slice of toast.

Peggy lamented the difficulty of keeping open the Wildlife Science Center. Based in Columbus, Minnesota, its mission is to save, study, and promote wild things, especially wolves. She's saved the genes of Mexican Wolves by keeping several animals at the center, she said, but getting contributions for their care had been almost impossible. It was much easier to acquire funding for a domestic dog rescue. "Every day the Science Center is a scrape, and they are an endangered species for crissakes. People care about what they connect with. I've had no problem feeding the abandoned dogs at home. What's left of home."

Breakfast, coffee, and discussion finished, Peggy loaded a few dogs into her pickup and put Megan in the car seat. I hopped into my own truck with Gretchen, who sighed audibly, relieved.

Leaving I-35 just above the Twin Cities, we turned off of county highway 18 into the Minnesota Department of Natural Resources' Carlos Avery Wildlife Management Area. We passed state buildings at the entrance and continued to the Wildlife Science Center. Founded by Ulysses Seal in 1976 with the help of David ("Mr. Wolf") Mech and other famous biologists, including Jane Packard, the site began as a wolf physiology project. It was a simple collection of kennels adapted for wolves who had been caught killing livestock. They were allowed a better fate than immediate termination. The idea was to let the animals live so that we could learn from them. Much less was known about their physiology at the time, and the team's results were crucial. The basic understanding of the effects of anesthesia and stress on wolves, essential for today's techniques, sprang from that little group of kennels in north central Minnesota. Macho field biologists of today wouldn't be jumping out of helicopters with ketamine-filled syringes without the work of physiologists at Carlos Avery.

An unlikely participant in the search for détente in the war on wildlife, Peggy completed a liberal arts education at Carleton College in 1984 and soon after joined the team as a wildlife technician. When Uly Seal retired in 1990, however, funding for the site rode into the sunset with him. Peggy, along with her then-coworker and soon-to-be husband Mark Beckel, saw the site's potential value for research and education. Rather than let the facilities and animals slip away, Peggy and Mark worked out a deal with the Department of Natural Resources to establish a nonprofit entity on the site, the Wildlife Science Center.

Peggy and I toured the facility, where my students would soon be measuring the responses of wolves and bears to new deterrent techniques and devices we were developing. While my thoughts were on animal behavior research, Peggy could see a bigger picture that I was just beginning to glimpse. The primary focus of the center was not methods development, but something much more important.

A yellow school bus pulled into the lot and a band of wild-eyed and unruly teenagers from the Twin Cities bubbled out. A few steps away, they met a pile of road-killed deer—wolf food. The students pointed at the carcasses and pinched their noses. They prodded and teased each other; their hip hop jewelry flashed and dangled. Their bodies were biologically primed and ready for independence, and they were testing limits constantly. The guidance and affection of their progenitors was no longer enough. Distractions and excitement erupted into loud repartees bandied back and forth enthusiastically. Frantic protestations from teachers and chaperones could not tame the teenagers. Their excitement was overstimulated by the novel environment and the potential for adventure. It seemed like an impossible crowd.

The interior of the center, where the pens were located, was blocked from view by an entrance building and gate. Out of sight, a mournful call began. Deep and growling, like tortured ghosts of the north woods, it grew. It permeated the buildings. It rang low through the weeds that invaded the gravel lot where we stood. It echoed into the high trees around us.

What adults could not do, wolves could: the teens grew quiet. A sound primeval, the call awakened something in their genes. Minds not yet cluttered by the logic and forward thinking of adulthood, teens feel strong tugs from simple biological drives either to reproduce, which they had been indirectly addressing moments before, or to survive. None of them had heard a wolf before, and the eerie sound focused their attention.

Peggy listened as the serenade wound down. Before the last, low rumble faded into silence, she used verbal judo to spin the crowd of students away from the calls of the wild and into the parlor of the entrance building. The room was decorated with thank-you notes and banners from previous visitors. A poster announced "Howl-een"—an opportunity to rest around a campfire, like our troglodyte ancestors did, and listen to the wolves' spooky chorus. There were wolf pelts draped over display cabinets, which were stuffed to overflowing with skulls, bones, and a menagerie of educational taxidermy.

"All right guys, we are here to see and talk about these animals."

Peggy did not open with a customary "May I have your attention?" She launched right into her presentation.

"And they aren't Timberwolves. In fact the only place you are going to see Timberwolves in Minnesota is on the basketball court." The connection had been made, effortlessly linking sports culture to the environment. "No, what we are going to talk about today are gray wolves."

She's brilliant, I thought. And with inner-city kids. As different from me as wolves are. And it is not about me at all, I realize. Anything I learn and develop is irrelevant if there is no one to connect with and no one who will care about and use the knowledge. *It is about them*, I thought—this will be the generation that will either learn to live with and tolerate our mammalian predators or not. But why should they care? How could they value a thing if they don't know it exists? It took contact, and that is what Peggy had made.

City kids would need to grow up with just a little connection to, and respect enough for, our predators to consider paying a little more for a hamburger, or eating one less. Who knows, any of these kids could grow up and move to the suburbs, or have a cabin in the woods that they'd have to guard from bears. It isn't enough to change the behavior of the animals. Perhaps it was too late for many of their parents, but young adults can be impressed and impacted by the beauty of wolves and other predators. They could be taught to respect our wolves, bears, cougars, and coyotes, rather than simply fear them, or worse, ignore them.

Peggy was flying around in front of the gaggle, dousing them with information as if she were splashing buckets of nature and wonder into the audience. Right in front of my eyes, she was changing perceptions. I stepped out and into the arena of the Wildlife Science Center and was surrounded by wolves once again. They walked gracefully to the edge of their pen and stared up at me, curious but cautious.

Animal advocates often lead appeals with emotion and crisis, and equally often end them with a "Take Action, Donate Now" button on the bottom of the web page.[1] That seems to be effective when preaching to the choir. To convince the agnostics, or otherwise elevate the argument, conservation-oriented scientists take a different tack. They present what are perceived as objective and irrefutable arguments in defense of species. They expound on grand ecological theories such as trophic cascades, using them to *prove* how important predators are in natural ecosystems. Ecologists assert that top predators are not only important but essential for providing top-down influence in ecosystems. The argument is that ecosystems can't function without carnivores. The only fix is to protect predators.

The problem: the basis of this supposedly scientific reasoning is not objective. The argument is imbued with a value set that has become so entrenched within the psyche of predator advocates that it doesn't feel like a collection of values or morals anymore. In actuality, many ecosystems have functioned for a long time without predators. Ecosystems without top carnivores look and act differently, but whether they ought to have—or lack—top predators is a subjective human value judgment. The argument that an ecosystem is only "correct" if it contains predators is meaningless to those with a different moral framework.

Another western bumper sticker reads, "Earth First! We'll log the other planets later." Why would someone with such a sentiment care about trophic cascades? Why would this person care about loss of species, other than species with economic value? Ecological arguments are irrelevant in such a context. All hope is not lost, however. The chasm between the various camps is not too wide to cross, but reaching solutions will require an acknowledgment of, and respect for, the idea that other values systems may be as valid as one's own. We must acknowledge our own internal biases too.

Perhaps "natural" ecological systems don't have any intrinsic value beyond what we assign them. The good news: even with die-hard resource extractors there can be a basis for agreement with the preservationist crowd. Ecosystems indeed have utilitarian value. Some people may enjoy the range in part because they can graze their cows over it and live from it. Others may enjoy it because it gives them a sense of awe, beauty, and spirituality. Both use and value the environment for their own purposes, just in different ways and to different degrees. Given a common point of reference at least, we can start communicating.

If we truly want to resolve the contradictions of the predator paradox, we ought to be studying the fears and perceptions of those who do not necessarily agree with us. We ought to walk a few miles in their shoes to understand what the relevant and effective arguments are.

Human perceptions, preconceived notions, and fear of the uncontrollable are not unique to North America. As Peggy worked to change perceptions of wolves among the next generation of young adults in Minnesota, a couple of Spanish conservationists were trying to change—or at least work within the context of—perceptions of predators in their own country. They came to me for help, but it wasn't clear to me what I could do, until I broadened my own perspective.

The Iberian Peninsula was spared much of Europe's historic environmental carnage, and many species that disappeared from the rest of the modern day European Union have persisted there. Spain has wolves, brown bears, and lynx. The peninsula is like an island, as geographically insulated by its rugged and narrow attachment to the continent as it had been politically isolated by Franco. During several work visits, I had the good fortune to see much of the country firsthand.

My series of collaborations with the Spanish environmental ministry at first seemed like an academic yawn—an applied and uninteresting question without grand ecological relevance. I soon learned that what seemed simple at first glance had a much deeper significance. Two Spaniards first visited the Predator Research Facility in the spring of 2005. Francisco García Domínguez was short and stocky, with a dark, Moorish countenance. I knew him by the common Spanish familiar *Paco*. At the time, my Spanish was nearly nonexistent, as was his English, and our tour of the facility was a Zen lesson in quietly accepting the moment and just observing. We met with Victor García Matarranz, who, like Paco, worked for Spain's central government's Servicio de Especies Amenazadas (Threatened Species Service). Victor's command of English helped considerably as I tried to understand the root of their efforts.

Victor was chiefly concerned with protecting eagles and black vultures. Paco focused on protecting the Iberian lynx. Together, we were creating a study of a new capture device for foxes, an effort I thought odd. They explained that in Spain, legal fox traps were needed to protect lynx, vultures, and eagles. At first I thought the gap in logic was due to some mistranslation.

I showed them different types of animal traps, scanning the same wall I had displayed to the congressional staff a few years before. They pointed out that anything with jaws would be illegal in the EU. In fact, most traps used in the United States were not allowed in Spain. I introduced them to the "Collarum." The device had U-shaped arms, which reclined flat against its base, and a little PVC tab protruding from a field goal position between the arms. A loop of cable snapped loosely onto the arms.

They marveled at it. Paco raised his thick eyebrows. "It is all buried except for this little tab that an animal bites on," I said, making my hand like a little mouth. I clamped my index fingers, representing incisors and thumb as lower jaw around the protruding piece. I showed how the spring would launch the arms up and propel the cable loop over a dog's head and around its neck. With some awkward fumbling, I pulled my arm away and the thick cable slipped effortlessly down to a small loop around my forearm. A clamped bit of ferrule stopped it from cinching too tight.

"It holds them like a dog on a leash with a collar."

¿Zorros?

"Foxes, exactly. Canids love to bite and pull on things. The good news is that a bear will swat and won't be caught. A ground squirrel could dig at it, I suppose, but if one did set it off, he'd just get catapulted across the field and not be slammed between jaws. This is really specific for canids and is a low injury way to do it."

Paco was very pleased.

I tried to understand why the device was so important. "So they can't use traps for foxes, but they can use this one. What does that have to do with lynx?"

"It's not the foxes," Victor said, struggling with the fine points of translation. "It's the people and what they use instead. It is illegal to use traps, so they find other ways to kill foxes. Cheap things that they can just put out."

Poisons, I surmised.

On my first visit to Spain, Paco and I drove around the Spanish countryside investigating potential study sites and meeting with collaborators. We passed through the great expanses of La Mancha, a verisimilitude of the plains of Wyoming. We found wolf tracks not far from town, even closer to livestock. We climbed into the peaks of the Pyrenees that jutted into the sky like the Sierra Nevada of eastern California. In the south, the hills of Andalucía were like the hillsides of coastal California, except that the bark of the Spanish oak was cork. Halfway around the world I found that differences were superficial, like language or tree bark. The core processes of people and ecosystems were the same.

We made our way to a great ranch called *La Garganta*. Arriving in time to start an early Iberian dinner at 10 p.m., we were seated among hundreds of antlers adorning the walls of an elaborate hunting lodge. Several bottles of wine into the meal, and after finishing with the spirit *aguardiente*, a man at the head of the table banged his fist on its surface. I sat quietly, timid as I was able to interpret only attitude and emotion. The man switched to English for one phrase only, to direct at me a derogatory remark about George W. Bush. No one offered to translate his other comments, but enough was clear from the tone of voice, the clenched jaw and fists.

I eventually learned the rancher was adamant that the only good fox was a dead fox. To him, Paco's arguments about eagles, vultures, or lynx were irrelevant. As long as foxes were being destroyed, it didn't matter if other things died. As in US predator control, they were considered collateral damage.

The crux of the matter, and the reason I was in Spain, was as convoluted as our journey from Madrid to Castilla y León to Andalucía and back. I had to understand the people to understand the problem.

The people wanted to manage their game, especially small birds and rabbits, and they feared fox predation. For generations they had hated the foxes, pesky animals that persisted across the landscape no matter how many they killed. Every country has its scapegoat and ignominious bastard of a varmint. In the United States, it is the coyote. In Spain, it is the red fox.

Spain looks like a country on a map, but its regional identities are strong, and its people fiercely independent. One doesn't mess with Andalucía or Catalan in the same way people are cautioned, "Don't mess with Texas." At dinner, the Andalucían rancher's vehement reaction was exactly the same as it would have been if we were in Texas, Wyoming, Montana, Maine, or many other states. People do not like being told what to do—or what not to do—whether the source is Madrid or Washington, DC.

A most primal of fears is the loss of power and self-determination. Subjugation. People who live off the land are especially passionate about their independence. Wind, rain, heat, and cold—there is so little over which they have control. It may look like arrogance to an outsider, but the reasons for the obstreperous-ness are deep. The attitude results from vulnerability, not hubris. When the locals feel that wolves or lynx, or anything, are being forced down their throats (the meaning, coincidentally, of the name of the ranch, *La Garganta*) they quietly take matters into their own hands. They want to solve their own problems.

There are hidden costs to wildlife laws, posing a complicated problem that we cannot simply legislate ourselves out of. Declaring jawed traps, as well as the act of trapping foxes, illegal in Spain had the ironic effect of creating not only lawbreakers, but an army of vindictive ones. They potentially spread unselective poisons that killed not only foxes but also lynx, eagles, and vultures. Thus the introduction of the Collarum was significant: the device was legal under EU law and it allowed people to feel like they were solving their own problems, yet it would not harm eagles or lynx.

Figuring out why the Spanish needed the Collarum seemed like a disjointed wander from cable restraint to fox to lynx and eagle, but why shouldn't the issue be so complicated? Lynx and wolves caused trophic cascades in their ecosystems. They caused emotional cascades in human social systems. Solutions to problems with wildlife will require nonlinear thinking and circuitous routes. They will necessitate establishing trust and cooperation through empowerment: giving things to the people you thought were the enemies, not merely taking more away from them.

Sandra Cavalcanti's PhD work in Brazil provides another example of the importance of perceptions. Her research proves that jaguars are far less of a threat than farmers think them to be.[2] Using hounds, trees, and tranquilizer darts, Sandra fitted GPS collars onto jaguars. She patiently collected 11,787 map points where the large cats wandered. Every now and then the cats would stop wandering, which translated into a cluster of points in the data. Such clumps indicated places where they had made a kill and then stopped to consume and digest it.

Sandra hiked to the locations where the data clustered and used the evidence she found at the site to determine what the jaguars had eaten. At nearly a third of the 415 kill sites, she determined that the prey was domestic beef. Livestock were found to be actually increasing the number of jaguars the environment could support. "In the Pantanal, cattle are both the most abundant and the most vulnerable prey, so some level of jaguar predation is an inevitable and a natural part of ranching, like drought or soil fertility," Cavalcanti and colleagues concluded. The impact of cattle on jaguars was large, but what was the impact of jaguars on cattle, stocked at sixteen cows per square kilometer (forty per square mile)?

The answer first depended on the jaguar. One adult male's diet was 55 percent beef. For another, a female, it was 49 percent. All the cats killed cattle, but three took only infrequent snacks, eating beef less than 15 percent of the time. Less than 3 percent of another adult male's diet was domestic livestock. A second adult female's diet included less than 5 percent livestock. Those cats preferred to nosh on the crocodile-like little caiman instead.

A second part of the answer depended on the ranchers. Dr. Cavalcanti and her colleagues examined the effects of predation more thoroughly in an insightful chapter in *The Biology and Conservation of Wild Felids.*[3] They proposed the "perception-blight" hypothesis, arguing that human persecution of jaguars was not necessarily related to the degree of depredation.

Indeed, surveys showed that jaguars were considered the most detrimental species to human livelihoods by 73 percent of 110 ranchers interviewed. The ranchers felt that they were being persecuted by the jaguars. It was emotional. Over all the ranches, the cattlemen estimated an 11 percent loss of their livestock to jaguars.

Those were the perceptions. What did the biology indicate? When Cavalcanti's team actually examined predation loss rates, it turned out that jaguars were responsible for 0.83 percent of loss in two ranches in the northern Pantanal. The cats took 0.3 percent of cattle from another ranch in the southern Pantanal, 1.26 percent in southern Amazonia, and 1.2 percent on Cavalcanti's study area. Thus, it was not the actual damage that was driving the cycle of persecution, but a blighted perception. It was the threat of damage. The fear.

In another ironic twist of perception back in the United States, statistics show that one may be more likely to be injured by a deer on the way to look for a grizzly bear in Yellowstone than to be hurt by a bear after getting there. Deer, especially white-tails in the east, fling themselves in front of 247,000 motor vehicles and injure or kill 26,647 drivers and occupants per year.[4] Yet for fish and game agencies, and the hunting public in many western states, the fear is that mule deer populations are actually disappearing.[5] This perception is also a problem for mammalian predators, especially cougars and coyotes, which dine on deer.

At the root of the issue with game populations is the scale of reference. In the bad old days of market hunting and unregulated killing of game, deer populations throughout the United States were nearly wiped out. In the 1920s, there may indeed have been only a few thousand deer in Utah and the surrounding states. After protective regulations, however, the herd grew exponentially, and there were about 500,000 mule deer in Utah alone by the mid-1950s. Then extreme winter conditions in 1992–1993 caused a tremendous die-off. Fewer than 250,000 animals remained there. The population has stabilized at a lower level, with yearly estimates of about 300,000 mule deer for every year of the last decade.[6]

Meanwhile, from 1920 to 2010, the human population in Utah rose from 449,396 to 2,763,885, and each generation has continued to build on crucial deer winter range. Between 1980 and 2010 alone, the number of humans in the state nearly doubled.[7] Given reductions in available winter habitat, it is not unreasonable to think that Utah's current herd is at carrying capacity—the environment is supporting as many deer as it has space and food for. However, if hunters remember 500,000 deer in the 1960s, and there are only 300,000 now, then someone has to do something about it. Right now.

What can be done? The houses and highways have been built, and more are on the way. Life-sustaining winter range for deer has been paved over. A harsh winter, like that of 1992, can decimate game populations, but we can't change the weather. Still, there is intense pressure to try to do something, anything that could help. So we kill coyotes, cougars, bears, and wolves.

One reflexive action in such situations is the use of bounties. Federal scientists and biologists have vehemently criticized bounties since the 1800s, but furor about predator damage to livestock and game tends to flare up intermittently.[8] Calls for bounties started again in Virginia in 1999 (with a hefty return of $50 to $75 per coyote depending on the county). As of 2003, bounties were legal in Colorado, Idaho, Minnesota, South Dakota, Texas, Utah, Virginia, and West Virginia.[9] Natrona County, Wyoming's Predator Management Board recently instituted a coyote bounty of $20 per coyote, to be paid out until the program's $10,000 budget is depleted.[10] The State of Utah took over a previous county-based bounty system in 2012. More than 7,100 coyotes were turned in for $50 each during the 2012–2013 fiscal year.[11] Utah ranks thirty-third per capita in school spending, but there are enough general tax dollars to allocate government payouts for general coyote removal.[12]

Ironically, research that evaluated the bounty program in Utah a decade ago questioned whether money actually motivated people to kill more coyotes. It concluded that since there were likely more than 100,000 coyotes in Utah, any effect of a program that removed less than 10 percent of the animals was not likely to help game or livestock operations. Indeed, the authors noted that "there is no documented evidence indicating that bounty programs temporarily or permanently reduce coyote abundance."[13]

Still, directed by the Mule Deer Protection Act, the State of Utah currently obligates $500,000 per year to be paid to people who submit coyotes for a $50 per coyote reward. Wildlife Services receives an extra $600,000 to gun coyotes from aircraft, an effort funded through a $5 fee attached to big-game licenses.

What do research studies conclude about the effectiveness of predator control for game protection?

The most extensive recent study was completed by Mark Hurley and colleagues with the Idaho Department of Fish and Game.[14] Their work was comprehensive and as scientifically rigorous as large-scale field studies go. Cougars and coyotes were targeted on four treatment game management units in southern Idaho, and four reference sites were used as controls.[15] Wildlife Services provided expert assistance. From 1997 through 2002, their specialists

and pilots removed 1,862 coyotes from the treatment units, at a total cost of $248,966. The average cost per coyote killed turned out
to be $135.95. How many deer did $135.95 per dead coyote create? Boiling the whole monograph into one succinct point, Hurley
and his colleagues concluded, "Winter severity in the current and
previous winter was the most important influence on mule deer
population growth." The cost of broad predator control did not
provide a return of investment in the form of more deer.

As shown in other studies, predator control may result in a
few more fawns surviving their first months, but rarely is a long-
term effect seen.[16] Limited by habitat, cold, and drought—and not
predators—fawns that aren't eaten die later that winter. No actual
increase in deer populations occurs. The phenomenon is called
compensatory mortality.[17] That is, many wild habitats where deer
now occur are more or less saturated, and a certain number are des-
tined to die every year. The proximate cause of death is irrelevant.
If coyotes do not kill the surplus fawns, the deer will die from other
causes, especially starvation or exposure.

Summarizing the literature, sometimes studies examining predator control do show a benefit—in certain, particular situations.
In more typical scenarios, however, control efforts tend to be ineffective.[18]

What is the scientific consensus, then, regarding predator control to protect deer? In short, the conclusion is that killing predators does not always and automatically create more deer. The best
available science recommends instituting predator control when
it can be shown that the unique circumstances exist where predators are limiting prey. This certainly happens, but is not always
the case. In addition, predator control should be done at a scale
small enough for predator populations to actually be impacted. For
coyotes, that requires repeated removal of 70 percent of the little
predators from a treated site, which is not an easy task unless the
area is small and tools are efficient and deadly.[19]

❦ ❦ ❦

If the effectiveness is dubious, why is so much money spent on
wide-scale predator control and on bounties?

The answers have to do with some little-recognized facts about modern wildlife management. First, wildlife management is public policy. How we manage wildlife is a function of what the people and their politicians desire and not necessarily a result of what biologists can do.

Also, in many states the primary mechanism for funding wildlife management—both game and non-game—comes from revenue generated primarily by hunting and related activities. Modern wildlife management was founded by hunting advocates in a more simple time, but the economic drivers have been retained. How we go about solving a problem is influenced by who pays for it. The historic funding source for most state wildlife agencies is consumptive users via hunting license sales. It shouldn't go unnoticed that one-third of state agencies in the United States use the word "game" in their title rather than "wildlife."

A huge source of federal funding is derived from hunting activities. The Federal Aid in Wildlife Restoration Act—more often referred to as Pittman-Robertson, alluding to its Nevada and Virginia sponsors—was signed into law by Franklin D. Roosevelt in 1937. The law created a tax on the sale of hunting equipment and dictated that the proceeds should be distributed as grants to the states for use on projects benefiting wildlife. Sportsmen do double duty funding wildlife management. There is no such mechanism other than state general funds to consistently pay for state management of non-game species and predators. The problem is in the eye of the purse holder, and if those that pay for wildlife management want more predators killed, why not?

Research indicates that campaigns to kill predators are biologically questionable or economically inefficient, so why are they created anew? There are a few reasons. Spread out over the populace, the tax implications are barely felt by individuals, but the concerted effort that can be mounted is large, and by some reasoning worth a try.

Another reason for the political inertia: to put it succinctly, sometimes it doesn't matter in the long run. Expenditures of time and money may be unlikely to increase deer populations, but equally important is that predator populations won't be impacted either. Guy Connolly's models showed that 70 percent of coyotes have to be killed to impact their populations, but Wyoming's and Utah's recent bounty programs could not have killed even 8 percent of them on the statewide scale. Biologically, such actions are often inefficient or irrelevant, but to human psychology the effect is priceless: finally someone is doing something to save the deer. And to give Utah credit, the state is closely monitoring coyote removals to determine how well the program is working.

Bounties may only be a predator placebo, an instance of biologically irrelevant psychological assuagement. But the placebo effect is real, and it makes people feel better. The role of politicians, if they want to be reelected, is to make people feel safer and happier. To assuage their fears. Perhaps biologists have something to learn from them.

We hunt our mammalian predators down, certainly, but their existence is ironically dependent upon our largesse, whether it is in the Brazilian Pantanal, the rural outskirts of Madrid, the pastures of Montana, or the irrigated heavens of our own urban-wildland interface. We love them and hate them, feed them and kill them, repulse them and attract them.

So is this an issue about the predators, or is it about the people? Which people? I found more similarities among rednecks in Spain and Wyoming than between urban and rural inhabitants of the same country. Who's to blame if a rancher feels cornered into a desperate need to kill a wolf? Is the responsibility, the blame, solely the rancher's? Is it only those people who live with predators nearby who must change? Or must the rest of us change too?

The problem cannot be solved by addressing only one component or perspective. Ensuring the continued survival of our great mammalian predators is largely a problem of communication, empowerment, and trust. The problem, with its many facets, requires a wide variety of approaches. Now that this is apparent, it is time to identify solutions.

PART II

DÉTENTE

CHAPTER 5

THE PHENOMENON OF FRIGHT
Disruptive Stimuli

As we launch into alternative methods of coexisting with predators—avoiding the quick trigger response of killing—we add layers of complexity to our efforts, both theoretical and practical. The first approach, using *disruptive stimuli*, is one that essentially relies on sabotage. Like throwing a shoe into some vast machinery to bring the whole process to a grinding halt, a minor disruption can break down complex systems. In our case, we want to break the chain of events that lead, stepwise, to a dead calf or lamb. As it turns out, there is far more to predation than eating meat. In life, death is certain, but the moment it comes is not. We can use the uncertainty to our benefit.

One of the most famous descriptions of the chain of events—or rather nonevents—on the path to predation was detailed by Dave Mech in his observations of moose within wolf striking-range at Isle Royale on Lake Superior.[1] Of the 160 moose he spied from the air, 29 weren't detected by nearby wolves. Step one of the predation process for the wolves was noticing the prey. Raising their noses, wolves pursued 120 of the moose, but 43 of the ungulates escaped before the wolves could even get close. Another 24 moose refused to run from the approaching wolves, a bold indicator of defensive strength, so the spindly but stoic ungulates were left alone. Of the 53 moose that wolves continued to chase, 34 outran or outlasted their pursuers, and only 7 were effectively attacked. Twelve others defended themselves aggressively and forced the predators to retreat. Of the whole lot of 160 potential meals, only 6 moose were actually killed. On the incremental path toward a feast, there was much more that went wrong than went right.

Predators have to detect, approach, pursue, evaluate, attack, and kill their prey. Any break in the chain, caused by just a small disruption, and there is no kill. We can use the phenomena of disruptive stimuli—sights, sounds, smells, or anything that causes a predator to startle or pause—to prevent predation.

The wolf is a master in his environment, but he is observant and wary, and not one to take chances. He remains stealthy and hidden with senses heightened beyond the imagination of olfactory-challenged primates such as us. His senses make him cognizant of occurrences over extraordinarily long distances and give him the gift of another type of fleeting communication, comparable to being able to read headlines on newspapers blowing in the wind. He can detect wafts of molecules on a gentle breeze and determine if a friend or foe approaches.

I think that wolves perceive the stench of human much as we recognize the odor of skunk, that the human signal has the same pungency over short distances and an equivalent piquancy when further away. Our footprints, certainly our constructions and litter, invade a wolf's consciousness like a flatulent parishioner among the pews of his church. Whatever the wolf thinks and feels, we will never truly know, but even human hunters from hundreds of years ago knew he desperately wanted to avoid us, even to the point of his undoing.

In the forests of eastern Europe, long after the development of gunpowder but far before the invention of helicopters, human hunters desired a certain improved efficiency in their killing of wolves. Technology allowed them to kill at a distance, but the stalk was still too difficult. The hunters set their minds to making their lives easier and making the wolves' lives shorter. They developed a technique for wolf hunting that was based on an ingenious application of ropes and rags strung through forests and snow-covered fields.

Kingly landowners would direct their subjects to string roped rags to create an immense funnel-shaped enclosure that narrowed toward a pit or corral. The men would start into the woods from the far end of the barrier and holler, drum, and march in line toward the exit. Wild animals within would dart and chase and collide with the boundary.

Deer would leap across the line and birds would fly over, incognizant of its existence, but wolves were different. The strange smells and sights in the strips of fabric, perhaps evidence of human, turned them. Unknowingly surrounded, they darted in fright only to encounter another virtual wall. They caromed from side to side, the path narrowing. At the enclosure's apex, they'd desperately dive into hemp nets that were camouflaged against a dark background of vegetation. Entangled, they were pinned and killed. Reports of people constructing these webs of nets and flags date as far back as 1639.[2] Such hunts became an upper-class sport.

Lines of flagging are today known as fladry, and they have been reincarnated for the recent pendulum swing: not for killing, but for conservation. Dr. Henryk Okarma and Włodzimierz Jędrzejewski, with the Polish Academy of Sciences, adapted the sport of Polish kings. They showed how the technique could be used to capture wolves and ready them for radio collars and subsequent studies of survival, instead of as a method for causing mortality.

The scientists worked along the edge of Belarus and Poland in a unique tract of ancient forest, the Białowieża Primeval Forest. Wolves still haunted the land, but they were wily and difficult to capture. Scientists and game wardens spread out in mechanized units to search the snow-covered ground for fresh tracks. Once the wolves' midday rest area was found, technicians lugged spools with 500-meter lengths of rope interspersed with colorful strips of cloth of many colors. Each strip, spaced by about a half a meter, was about 30 cm long and half as wide. Using the system, they roped off the surrounding area, about a kilometer in diameter (0.4 square miles). Ready, the scientists and rangers formed a line within the barrier against its far, closed end and counted back and forth loudly as they marched to create a pursuing barrier of commotion.

At the narrow end, they slung fishing nets from the trees. Confused and frightened wolves hit them at a gallop and dragged the nets off of loose anchors. The combination of wolf and net rolled into a tangled ball, and the animals were pinned and sedated.

The scientists practiced the process on five different occasions, with varying numbers of people to harass the wolves. Their least successful attempt occurred with a line of four people. Fourteen seemed to be about optimal for driving wolves into the nets. In all, fourteen to sixteen wolves were encircled. Most wolves were herded successfully, but not all wolves responded equally. One escaped by scooting under the fladry, and another broke out by jumping over it.

Intrigued by the success of the Polish researchers, Marco Musiani and Elisabetta Visalberghi, then with the Psychology Institute in Rome, delved further into the phenomenon, bringing it to the attention of the rest of Europe. And, rather like a modern day pair of Christopher Columbi, they piloted the concept to the New World via the pages of the *Wildlife Society Bulletin*.[3]

With five captive wolves in two pens at the Rome Zoo, they tried various conditions and fabrications of fladry in the hopes of further optimizing its effectiveness. They exposed wolves to fladry hanging high and low, and even laid it on the ground at the wolves' feet. Sometimes flags were red, sometimes gray. Sometimes the scientists used an aluminum rope. They moved the flags closer or farther apart. Some flags were rigid and inserted into the ground. For controls, they stuck pipes in the ground or just dug small holes. They used eighteen different combinations to determine which composed the best virtual barrier for keeping wolves from favorite areas of their pens.

Wolves passed when the flags were a meter apart, especially when the ropes were strung high. Even less effective were the controls of holes in the ground or fladry laying on the surface. Wolves even seemed to like the pipes, frequently investigating the poles that stood in a line across their paths. In contrast, the most repulsive constructions were fladry as it had been traditionally strung for centuries, red or gray, and suspended half a meter high.

Marco and Elisabetta showed the effect of a promising technique. It wasn't even a fence or physical barrier that kept the wolves at bay. It was a virtual barrier, something that was symbolic to the wolf and raised the fear within them. It was a bluff, but it worked.

Alex Mettler had curly hair cropped like Michelangelo's *David* and a smile as mischievous and bright as the *Mona Lisa*'s. His art could be described as a study of primary colors animated in multidimensional space: red flags on blue twine waving in the breeze. Fladry had arrived in America and Alex was introducing it to coyotes. The first step was to determine if coyotes were also susceptible to the juju of the flagging.

At the Predator Research Facility, he had the benefit of working with far more experimental subjects than Musiani or Visalberghi had, so his questions were more complex. Good science does not just ask *yes* or *no*, but tries to understand *why*. How would living in social groups affect coyote responses to frightening stimuli? By definition, dominants eat first when paired with a subordinate animal. It stands to reason, then, that subordinates would generally be more hungry and motivated to obtain food. Alex's hypothesis was that subordinates would be bolder when encountering disruptive stimuli because they have to be. They need to be more willing to take chances when an opportunity arises. But how strong is dominance? If dominant individuals bully the subordinates away from food, would fladry protect food from the dominants, who then would keep hungry subordinates away from the protected area?

This force multiplier idea highlights one of the best arguments for using nonlethal techniques in predator management. When animals are lethally removed from an area of conflict, social structure and interactions are also impacted. New predators almost immediately replace the previous, and the gap before reinvasion may only be a few weeks.[4] A stable system can be managed, but if a system is in unpredictable flux it is much more difficult to do so.

Because of the way they disrupt social structure, lethal techniques may actually exacerbate human-wildlife conflicts. If a pack of coyotes or wolves, or a tom cougar—for reasons of variability, personality, or culture—is not killing livestock, its dominance over the territory excludes other predators and thus prevents losses. New, and thus more desperate, animals with the proclivity to cause conflict can't intrude. Social canids do this, as do male cougars[5] and perhaps male bears. Leaving predators in their territories repels other, often worse ones. The irony makes biologists chuckle: *guard coyotes.*

Alex Mettler strung fladry around a small, square area within paired coyotes' pens. He dropped morsels of food into the protected area and then observed his subjects. His first hypothesis was that coyotes would not cross the virtual barrier, just like their wolf cousins. A second hypothesis was that subordinate coyotes would be more motivated to overcome the fright of fladry. If frightening stimuli broke down social order just as lethal removal did, would it work any better? It was a question that had to be asked, too.

Step one was easy. Indeed, coyotes avoided the areas protected by fladry. Only two in twenty eventually overcame the repellency and rushed past the barrier.[6] Nothing is perfect, but the effect was clear: fladry worked for most coyotes, and it repelled both the dominant and subordinate animals. Pushing the limits of the effect, Alex exposed the coyotes to fladry for days at a time and observed how they habituated. Would the subordinates dash past first?

The results were encouraging. Dominant coyotes approached the strings of fladry more than subordinates did. They were more persistent, darting closer to gather information and learn. Ultimately, the dominant coyotes were bolder, and for the nine pairs that entered the protected zone, the initial intruder was the dominant individual.[7] For a while at least, the dominant was afraid of the fladry, and subordinate wary of the dominant.

There *could* be guard coyotes.

The Critter Gitter is a little black box about the height, length, and thinness of a writer's wallet. Designed to startle and repel deer from backyard gardens, it is small and relatively inexpensive, running on nine-volt batteries.[8] Its construction is mostly of black plastic, but it has a fogged-white lens on its forehead. Red LEDs sit on either side of the frosted detector cover, and a round opening gapes like a howling mouth below the little lights. Hidden under the opaque plastic is an infrared motion detector, not unlike the ones that open grocery store doors when a shopper approaches. When a warm body moves in front of a Critter Gitter, the red lights flash and the box wails loudly.

The inexpensive little item is not the answer to all of our woes, but it is an example of available technology that ought to be incorporated into modern wildlife management—an alternative to grabbing a gun first. Not rocket science, just an inventive application of parts that can be found in a local electronics store. It is already something that can be positioned in a back yard to frighten away coyotes or foxes—or deer for that matter. Can we end the war on our predators just by stringing a few flags and applying some car alarm technology?

Critter Gitters sat perched over piles of coyote treats at the Predator Research Facility. Nervous coyotes paced around them. Some dodged in to look for an opening. Upon finding none, they jumped back. Others avoided the black box altogether. Video cameras recorded them all.

My study design was straightforward. Forty-two coyotes in twenty-one pairs divided into three experimental groups. I suspended Critter Gitters two meters above the door to the pen and, to begin a trial, dropped a plop of coyote food below the device. Coyotes were sure to be hungry too, having been fasted a day before testing.

The question at hand involved examining three different ways to present such disruptive stimuli. The first, a control, was an easy modification. Those Gitters were quiescent, turned off. They hung silently, like miniature black scarecrows. The second group was composed of Critter Gitters installed as recommended. If a coyote moved in front of one, the device would flash and wail. The third bunch of Gitters was rewired. Their motion detectors were bypassed and the energy routed through a capacitor instead. The modified devices activated periodically, averaging about seven seconds of wailing and five seconds of quiet. My hypothesis was equally simple: coyotes would habituate differently, depending upon the versions of the Critter Gitter to which they were exposed.

The simple, silent sentries in the control group were as effective as any common scarecrow. That is to say, coyotes didn't avoid them for long. Initially wary of a novel object, because they are coyotes after all, they first approached slowly. They approached and nothing happened. A little closer, and still nothing happened. It was not long before they learned that there was no threat, and they eagerly lowered their heads to eat. All of the coyotes in the control group ate.[9]

The devices that wailed regularly were a bit more effective. The bright and noisy object stood out from the environment, its signal blaring against the peaceful background of the pen. Some coyotes simply decided that the lights and noise were too spooky, and they refused to eat. But for other animals, the disturbance did not continue as a barrier. With every activation, the wail became just more irrelevant noise in the environment. The siren soon became no more alarming than the rustle of wind over grass. It wasn't long before it stopped working—71 percent of the coyotes in that group ate and less than 30 percent continued to be repelled. Better than nothing, but far from perfect.

The final group, however, provided the most important results. The off-the-shelf Critter Gitters had working sensors that commanded the device based on movements of an approaching coyote. The lights and sounds were the same as with the intermittently activating devices. The results were dramatically different, however, because the behavior-contingent activation repelled more than 80 percent of the coyotes during the study.

In a practical context, the difference between the intermittently activating and the behavior-contingent devices is minimal. One flashed lights and pierced the air with its siren. The other did the same. How the device was activated, however, made all the difference. It was indicative of something much bigger, and hinted at concepts that would need to be understood if we were to effectively apply all of our bells and whistles in fields and forests.

For all animals, the world is a constant bombardment of sights and sounds, touches, tastes, and odors. There is so much coming at them that their problem of perception is not really determining what to pay attention to, but rather figuring out what to filter out. An animal's perpetual challenge is to sort out what is relevant and important—or in biological terms, *salient*—from all of the extraneous noise that surrounds them. A gentle wind is irrelevant unless it carries the scent of friend, foe, or food. A tree is not important in its existence, but in what it hides. How does one choose what deserves attention?

Animals suffer through their own paradox of having to balance simultaneously two opposing motives: needing to learn about and take advantage of the world around them while not being killed by it. Every action is like considering whether or not to walk across a frozen pond. The ice can be a bridge to new opportunities or, in breaking, can cause their death. The problem is that they have to step toward the middle before they know which fate awaits them. If they are able, they will bide their time and gather information from a safe distance. They'll use the buffer of time and space to determine whether novel stimuli, such as strange light or sound, are dangerous or not. This is to say, predators are motivated to learn and to outsmart our efforts. Our challenge is to determine how to keep a frightening device salient for as long as possible.

Habituation is an active learning process in which animals find out that a stimulus, even a loud one, is irrelevant and harmless. To maintain the effectiveness of disruptive stimuli, such a realization has to be prevented. A siren wailing every five minutes is disruptive, but it dooms itself because of its predictability. A thing can't be startling if an animal knows it is coming. Adding an element of randomness reduces predictability, which prevents learning and habituation. Randomness can occur through variations in lights or sounds, changes in location, or activation at irregular intervals. Finally, there is behavior-contingent activation—using a motion detector or other such trigger.

There are additional observations worth noting about the studies in this chapter and, indeed, all of the studies described in this book. The crux of the matter, however, comes down to a necessary admission and admonition: First, some devices and approaches are better than others. The cleverest Critter Gitter frightened away most of the coyotes, and the silent ones were worthless. More important to acknowledge, however, is that even if we throw all the theory and practice at them, living predators still must eat. Repelling more than 80 percent of the coyotes is pretty good, but it isn't 100 percent. You can fool some of the predators all of the time, but not all of the predators all of the time.

❧ ❧ ❧

Edward Cummings's voice drawled through the phone, carried from his ranch in the Bitterroot Mountains of Montana. It was early spring at the beginning of the twenty-first century, and Ed's cows were about to start calving. A wolf had just been caught, unexpectedly, in a coyote trap near his property and that of his neighbor, Tom Ruffatto, a situation that was truly frightening for Ed. The local joke is to invoke the three *s*'s in such a situation: shoot, shovel, and shut up. Doing the right thing instead, the trapper alerted the authorities. Federal biologists had radio-collared the young wolf and turned it loose.

Ed wasn't calling to complain or launch into a stereotypical tirade. Rather, he was trying to make it clear that it wasn't just that wolves were around that was the problem. The problem was that they killed cattle. Stating that fact may have drawn hate in some circles and applause in others, but the reasoning was nonpartisan. As long as the wolves weren't killing his calves, so what if they were around? But having a wolf that close to the pastures was asking for trouble. Ed brainstormed with the biologist. The rancher wanted to know if there was some way that his and his neighbor's cows could be protected from the threat.

Ed made the point that there was a radio collar on one of the wolves now because of the serendipitous actions of a coyote trapper. An educated man, like most of today's ranchers, Ed surmised that there must be some way that the technology of radio waves, transmitters, and receivers could change the playing field. If we could collar and track a wolf, it should certainly be possible to keep it out of a pasture. A Montana rancher's musings provided the spark for the next generation of approaches to keeping predators away from areas where we don't want them. It was another example of how diversity of thought—and willingness to listening to others—is a prerequisite for innovation.

In my laboratory sat sleeping a relic of the 1980s, a cylinder of white PVC wearing a strobe light like a cap. It was known as an Electronic Guard and was designed to frighten away coyotes. The electronics were vintage 1980s Radio Shack and included a light sensor, but other than that they were pretty dumb, especially by today's standards. The device was simple in design, incorporating little more than a strobe light, siren, timer circuit, and light sensor, all powered with a 12-volt lantern battery. When the sun slipped under the horizon, the device would intermittently activate its strobe and siren. In place in the pastures, the devices sort of made it look like UFOs were landing, while the sounds made it seem as if law enforcement was arriving. Several such devices moved around sheep bedding grounds kept coyotes at bay. The method worked, and it had been shown to reduce coyote kills on sheep, especially when several devices were employed.[10]

Outside, someone nudged a car in the parking lot. A car alarm responded to the intrusion and whooped in protest. What we needed was a car alarm for wolves. The Electronic Guard was resting silently in my laboratory, its electronics dated. It was time for an upgrade.

I obtained a scanning radio receiver and enlisted the assistance of Gene Bourassa, a colleague and electronics guy, who put together a simple circuit that I could hook from the Electronic Guard into the headphone jack of a scanning radio receiver. If the circuit "heard" a loud noise (the beep of an approaching wolf collar) the device would activate. Thus was born the Radio Activated Guard. I threw the green army surplus box that protected the receiver and the car battery that powered it into the back of a truck and rolled toward Missoula. Carter Niemeyer of *Wolfer* fame,[11] who was then the wolf specialist for Wildlife Services, met me and brought me to the edge of Tom Ruffatto's pasture. Pressed into service as the youngest and most agile in the group, I climbed a few stories up a tree to suspend the rewired cylinder to listen for wolves. The concept soon became known by its acronym: the RAG box.

Returning to the ground, I let the coaxial cable hang down the trunk. I tuned the receiver as Carter and the rancher tested the boundary; it was unclear whether they were impressed or amused by the clumsy wiring. Nonetheless, the components did what they were supposed to do. When the two approached the edge of the pasture with an activated collar, the device responded.

There was no treatment and no control, and the application was far from scientific proof. But two things happened: First, there were no calves killed that season. Second—and more important— the ranchers slept better at night knowing that someone was on guard, that someone was doing something.

Rick Williamson replaced Carter Niemeyer as Wildlife Services wolf specialist after Carter's bitter departure.[12] Rick was an avid supporter of the Radio Activated Guard and other nonlethal techniques for wolf management. Not so tall as he was large, Rick appeared better suited for sitting down and chewing the fat with ranchers than climbing into the back of a Piper Cub to dart wolves. But it was his easy manner and desire to interact with folks that was so important. He had to stay calm around angry people.

Rick's conclusions came with the reasoning that the more tools he had, the more he could do for people. Doing nothing was not an option when wolves were at the door—even when there was nothing he could do. Doing something, anything, meant he would be perceived as helpful by his constituents, the local ranchers.

In my personal experience, most Wildlife Services specialists were tolerant and polite about research, but a scientist could not shake the feeling that the operations guys generally concluded that most research was frivolous. It was as if they felt that research existed to appease and distract the environmentalist, but wasn't something actually to be implemented.

The operations guys were smart problem solvers, too, and they knew how to invent the things they needed anyway. I frequently joked that if you gave government trappers a bit of car bumper, they'd figure out a way to bend it into something they could catch a coyote with. Many of them really are that good, but they hold certain biases, too. It was difficult, on both sides, to make the connection from metal springs to the nonlethal rocket science I was toying with.

My general perception was that many of the specialists felt that they already knew how to solve the problem—bullets were cheap and easy—but there was more to the disconnect. Alternative methods, such as electronic guards, could make them uncomfortable, even fearful, because anything different was a threat to a way of life and livelihood. Anything that threatened the right to kill was an affront, an attack on a fundamental right, a dismissal of who was in charge. To an agency that had been fighting a war on wildlife for several generations, nonlethal approaches to resolving conflict between man and wolf were powerful symbols of coming demise. Again, it was a fear of losing one's way of life. But agencies are composed of people, and even Wildlife Services' uniformed employees are not uniform in approach and opinion. One must be careful not to generalize or stereotype, I learned.

Rick Williamson, an unlikely iconoclast, was eager to use whatever our lab could produce. He also was careful to make observations and keep records. I supplied a few RAG boxes for him, and we were able to gather observations from animals in the field.

Early spring in Idaho is much like the depths of winter in other parts of the United States, but to be ready for the lush green-up of spring, livestock producers often time their calf production as early as they can. If their calves are ready for slaughter before their competitor's calves glut the market, they can demand a higher price per pound. If they are too early, spring storms and subfreezing weather could kill the young calves and jeopardize the whole year. Wolves, of course, add another layer of risk, complexity, fear, and discomfort.

In January 2000, Rick installed a RAG box in a pasture, much like I had a year before, but by that time his was much prettier and easier to use.[13] It was designed and built by engineers I found at a little company called Avian Systems out of Louisville, Kentucky.

Avian Systems got into the business to sell devices that would frighten birds away from airfields. Protecting billions of dollars worth of aircraft and millions of human lives was much more lucrative than defending a couple cows, so it took some convincing that the niche market of managing mammalian predators was worth the effort.

They added some improvements to my initial prototype. Introducing a degree of unpredictability to the noise stimuli, the device looped an audio tape that switched sounds. Sometimes a man yelled "Heyaaa! Heyaaa!" and banged a low-pitched cow bell. At other times, the sound of a helicopter swooped in, followed by the slamming of pins in a bowling alley. There was also the sound of screeching tires, shattering glass, and crunching metal of a car crash. It sounded like the world was coming to a very confused end.

Rick had collared wolves in packs near livestock and knew that there was indeed a threat. The pack aspect of wolf behavior is a benefit, because just one or two radio collars can be used to monitor, and frighten away, an entire group. To evaluate the effectiveness of the system, I wired a data logger into the RAG, which recorded when the device activated. We also added an additional scanning receiver that monitored the airwaves and recorded when the pack visited. We would know when wolves were in the area and when they approached close enough to activate the disruptive lights and sounds.[14]

No kills were observed initially, although the rancher had noticed the device going off on one or two occasions. Through a little investigative work, we put the pieces together. Yes, wolves had come. They had approached the pasture slowly and cautiously. They eventually came close enough to activate the RAG, and immediately fled just as they were supposed to. The surprise is what they did next.

Rick milled around a little to survey the situation. The snow was fresh and good for tracks. He walked the perimeter of the pasture to search for clues. He found them. The evidence was written in the snow as clearly as if by pen on paper. At least one wolf had approached. The pack moved efficiently, single-file, foot-track to foot-track, and many appeared as one. The confident lope lasted only until they reached the limits of the pasture. Then, they suddenly scattered in disarray and galloped away.

Rick knew that for wolves, life is about persistence and learning, so he continued following their tracks. The signs in the snow showed they had regrouped, but they did not return directly. Instead, they circled. They ducked behind a nearby hill and came at the pasture from another side, trying to outflank the RAG. Noises and lights activated a second time, and the wolves fled from the area.

In late February, about half of the approximately 350 cows were moved with their calves into a second, unprotected pasture. The next night, a calf was killed in the unprotected pasture, and five more were killed during the next week. No other RAGs were available to protect that pasture, so lethal control was implemented. Radio collars can be used to find wolves, too, and within days there were four dead wolves and no Twin Peaks pack.

The next year, Rick made similar observations along the east fork of the Salmon River. He did not have enough boxes to cover the whole valley. Although five RAGs were placed, only about 70 percent of the pastures in the area could be protected from the nearby White Hawk pack. In one unfortunate night, March 18, 2001, the scanning receiver was not turned on, and wolves walked within twenty meters of the inactivated box. They killed a calf. After the device was fixed, wolves continued to visit, but were repelled. They visited at least twenty more times without making kills until April, when the pack left the valley.

When people consider the whoops and wails of alarms and the thudding of the simulated helicopters and gunfire, often a thought strikes them: Loud noises will keep ranchers or shepherds up at night—could there be selective sounds that would not bother people, yet would be particularly terrifying to canids, felids, and ursids? If you've thought of ultrasound, you are not alone.

Why don't we have an ultrasonic guard? Actually, we do. A cousin to the Critter Gitter is the YardGuard.[15] It features a motion detector and is rated to project a 15,000 to 25,000 Hz signal at 90 dB a meter away. Does it work any better than a conventional device?

The YardGuard will repel deer, the principle target for suburban gardeners. We don't have more ultrasonic repellents, however, because the invisibility does not come for free. There are technological barriers. To startle and disrupt, sound has to actually be loud, immediate, and, at its best, annoying. It is technically difficult and relatively more expensive, however, to generate and radiate sound greater than 130 dB, especially in high frequencies. The natural environment is not a concert hall; every swale of earth and growth of tree and vegetation gathers and absorbs sound waves, clipping especially the peaks and valleys of high-frequency waves. Audible and lower sounds travel better in air and remain louder, and are therefore more effective than ultrasound. Hence, ultrasound has potential benefits in not disturbing people, but it is more difficult to reach as far. It can seem too good to be true, so wishful customers should recognize the limitations of all tools.[16]

What will our frightening devices of the future look like? With enough money and devotion, anything can be done. I am certain that given Air Force surplus drones we could monitor every wolf from Wisconsin to Wyoming in the comfort of a heated trailer at Hancock Field. Unmanned aircraft could be part of the solution one day, but more measured and direct responses are here now.

We know a lot about what would constitute the best disruptive stimulus device. It would have several key components: it would activate only when predators approach, and it would be multisensory, so that the animals would not rapidly habituate to its components.

Let's add other options too. Our device would produce salient sights and sounds—even odors that predators would recognize not as smells of the forest, field, or prey, but as biological signals of potential trouble or danger. It would be movable, fully automatic, self-propelled, and capable of following a herd or flock as it ranged through the grasslands. It would have all of this, yet the electronics would be simple enough that people would not need an advanced degree in electrical engineering or computer science to operate it. It would be relatively inexpensive. Our invention wouldn't need batteries that needed to be replaced constantly.

We've just built a guard dog.

Guard dogs make noise and smell, and they patrol. They need food and some maintenance, but not advanced guidance systems. There are many breeds that have already stood the test of time, especially Great Pyrenees, Akbash, Anatolian shepherds, and Komondors. All are large and white and stand out from the environment rather prominently. There is certainly nothing new about them in the Old World, and they are becoming more common in some parts of the American West, with Great Pyrenees the favorite for guarding sheep.

The approval ratings for guard dogs in Colorado suggest that they could soundly defeat any incumbent president; 91 percent of sheep producers rate their dogs' performance at reducing predation as good or excellent.[17] Statistics reported in various studies from the 1980s and 1990s indicated that dogs saved thousands of dollars in sheep annually, an average of $3,216 per producer.[18] About two-thirds of the dogs tested reduced the number of attacks per year, and one-quarter of them reduced attacks on sheep from more than six per year to zero. There is indeed something to these animals and their perfect application of behavioral theory.[19]

Expectations must be managed, of course. Some dogs are better than others. They must be imprinted on sheep: raised as pups and surrounded by the animals that they will grow to protect. In a clever twist of interspecies relations, if done right, sheep see the dog as a herd member, while the dog sees sheep as pack members. Not all dog breeds, or individual dogs, have the temperament to do this.

There are financial costs associated with using guard dogs. Initial investment may be upwards of $1,000 dollars, and subtle changes in husbandry may be necessary, including provisioning the dogs with self-feeders, but after the first year the costs of maintaining guard dogs drops by about three-quarters.

Don't discount the cleverness of wolves and coyotes, though. Coyotes will lure one guard away while another coyote makes a kill. They can be that wily. With two good and compatible guard dogs, if one chases a coyote, the other can still maintain a presence near the flock. There are other limits, too: one dog is no match for a wolf or bear. As Tom Ruffatto says, "They just look at those big guard dogs as wieners-on-a-stick."[20] Multiple guards, selected for strength and aggressiveness, may be required to improve effectiveness against species that are bigger and meaner than coyotes.

For repelling coyotes, there are other living options that will send the little canids running. Most donkeys have an innate hatred of canids and will bray, chase, kick, stomp, and bite at them.[21] Donkeys are natural herd animals and don't require different food, like dogs would, but they will act as effective guards against coyotes. It is important to use only one jenny or a gelded jack, because two of the same species will wander off together rather than bond with the sheep or goats they are placed to protect. Donkeys may not be as effective as guard dogs, but they are much cheaper and easier to employ.

Llamas share the hatred of canids and are also beloved among the sheep producers that have used them, with a 90 percent approval rating in one study.[22] If sheep producers used them one year, they were using them the next. Although llamas' effectiveness is reported to be limited to bands of 200–300 sheep in open fields, 94 percent of those surveyed considered them an effective method of reducing sheep loss to predators.

Another potential guard animal is *Homo sapiens*. A good herder who stays with and guards livestock can be an effective method of protection. We can't smell wolves on the wind like guard dogs can, but we can maintain electronic devices and noisemakers, and use human ingenuity to disrupt the advances of predatory species. Sheep producers tend to import herders from South America to watch over their flocks, but typically still need dogs to help repel wily coyotes at night. The mere presence of people may be more repellent to wolves and beneficial in cattle operations, but the expense of paying experienced people to ride the range at night is a difficult hurdle to overcome without significant economic input.

With charismatic species like wolves, human herders—some even volunteers—are an option. The Defenders of Wildlife has sponsored such efforts for years. Beginning in 2008, Defenders sent technicians into central Idaho to watch over more than ten thousand sheep that move through the Sawtooth Wilderness. They used guard dogs, portable fencing, starter pistols, flashlights, and air horns to keep wolves away, and reported fewer than twenty sheep lost—attributing most predation to times when their guards were not present.[23]

◤ ◤ ◤

With alternatives such as guard dogs, Radio Active Guards, fladry, llamas, and many other methods that we will soon explore, why do we continue an almost exclusively lethal war? Why don't we use a greater variety of available methods? I have less scientific data to use in answering these questions, but I have made certain observations about human and bureaucratic nature.

Ironically, in the 1970s and 1980s Wildlife Services (then known as Animal Damage Control) investigated guard animals.[24] The agency developed and marketed, in a very limited way, Electronic Guards too.[25] The devices even used to be available for purchase through the agency's Pocatello Supply Depot, but no longer. We have backslid from the environmental optimism of the 1970s.

Today, Wildlife Services employs a theoretical decision model that compels the agency to act with lethal force by concluding beforehand that other methods and approaches probably won't work.[26] It is the easy route, a literal case of shoot first, don't bother to ask questions later. Status quo. But there are other complexities. In the simplest and most cynical interpretation, guard dogs take away specialists' jobs, in a kind of interspecies outsourcing. Is the world leader in animal damage management unable to actually implement novel methods and technologies because of a fear of becoming irrelevant?

I must give the agency and its people the benefit of the doubt here. There are many people within Wildlife Services who are certainly doing what they do because they want to help people. They kill things because they care. I have met many employees and have extraordinarily high respect for them. I support them as far as their mission goes—to minimize conflicts between humans and wildlife. Given bureaucratic realities, however, there is a certain amount of inertia involved. As evident in the agency's tables and lists, we know how to kill predators. Wildlife Services does this exceptionally well, and there will always be resistance to change, especially in multigenerational bureaucracies.

Guard dogs can complicate matters. If a neighbor has dogs and a rancher wanting help from Wildlife Services does not, using lethal tools can be risky. One beloved lethal tool is the M-44 cyanide ejector. It is designed for canids, because animals have to bite and pull to activate it (much like the Collarum). Its specificity for canids was one of the attributes that allows its current use. Although most toxins had been banned by President Nixon, the M-44 was quickly reinstated by President Ford.[27]

When a dog grips an M-44 with its mouth, the device activates and a wad of cyanide powder is propelled onto its tongue. The powder mixes with saliva and cyanide gas is formed and inhaled. Death is rapid. Guard dogs and pets are as susceptible to the M-44 as coyotes are. Because of the strong reliance on lethal methods as the first choice, the presence of guard animals means a limitation of options for the Wildlife Services specialist, not an expansion of them.

Incorporating guard animals, disruptive stimuli, and other nonlethal methods that we will discuss into the panoply of tools of first resort will take time.

CHAPTER 6

PERSONALITY AND PEER PRESSURE

How do coyotes decide when and where to hunt? The question was the basis of Lynne Gilbert-Norton's research on how coyotes think—specifically, how they think about food. To survive, coyotes had to find carcasses, watermelons, calves, fawns, lambs, and rabbits. Locations of food had to be learned and plotted in cognitive maps. Lynne couldn't see the neural connections or interview the coyotes, obviously. To study the animals' abilities, Lynne devised mind games that pit her against the epitome of cleverness.

Lynne wanted to figure out how coyotes learned about food, about its presence and the rhythms of abundance. Sometimes a carcass appears on the side of a road, which makes areas around roads good places to forage, but exactly if, when, and where a carcass appears is not predictable. So it is with house cats in the suburbs or deer fawns in the fields. There are areas of higher and lower probability, but few places that will always provide a certain meal. Lynne was studying how coyotes navigate that curious area between predictability and non-predictability.

There was real-life importance to the work, too. Did the routine nature of livestock husbandry methods predispose some domestic animals to predation? Could coyotes learn to predict pet food locations and use that knowledge to successfully invade suburbs? Alternatively, some sorties could get coyotes killed. High speed cars give, but they can also take away. How did coyotes learn to optimize their behavior and survive at the interface of the human world?

Lynne designed an experiment in which coyotes were fed at different times and in different places in their pens, without any obvious human connection or cause. To create the study, she developed programmable automatic coyote feeders. They weren't something you'd find on the shelves of Home Depot or Pet Smart, so she had to be innovative. She adapted some programmable fish feeders, little battery powered devices designed to drop pellets of fish food into commercial ponds at scheduled intervals. With the addition of duct tape, Tupperware hoppers, a ten-gallon protective bucket, and wooden four-by-fours, Lynne created stand-alone feeders in several pens. Towering over the feral alfalfa ground cover, they looked like lanky and lonely R2-D2s.

🖤 🖤 🖤

Initial results were straightforward. Food availability, be it dropped randomly or in a predictable way, influenced coyotes' behavioral patterns. When the food source was predictable, the coyotes became lazy. They rested more. The others—animals given the unfortunate predicament of not knowing when food would come—grew stressed. Those coyotes spent more time patrolling and marking their territory, peeing to mark boundaries and howling to indicate possession.[1]

The results meant that food availability and distribution was linked to such seemingly disparate behaviors as howling and peeing around a boundary. Coyotes were not walking, unthinking stomachs. They would alter their strategies depending on the environment in which they found themselves. This meant that predator management would require understanding the suite of interconnected behaviors related to food.

The next research step utilized fish feeders again, but it also involved a more in-depth investigation of learning. Coyotes were clever, but how clever were they? Could they count, track resources, and then use that ability to optimize their foraging? Lynne's hypothesis was that coyotes were like ten-year-olds at Halloween: avoiding the poor or less generous neighborhoods and spending most of their evening on Mansion Avenue, where the treat bowls were deepest.

To do the work, more inventions were needed. Lynne created

coyote foot pedals. ("Not bad for someone who is mechanically inept," she joked.) Coyotes love to pounce, and it is a joy to watch them use their ears to triangulate the location of a vole under the snow. They launch upwards and onto the rodent, flattening it between their two front paws before snapping it up. Lynne's idea was to use the pounce behavior to measure motivation, but instead of pouncing on mice for a treat, they would stomp their feet on the lid of little plastic boxes. The truly clever bit was Lynne's: she designed the devices and programmed the computer interface so the pedals would click, count, and alter food rewards for her purposes. The games could begin.

Lynne programmed some boxes to reward only after many coyote stomps. She programmed others with varying degrees of generosity. During the next few months, she ran trials with her rout of coyotes, observing and measuring how they responded to each pedal and packet of food.

In short, as Lynne's paper on the subject in the journal *Behavioural Processes* reported, "Results showed all coyotes efficiently tracked changes in reinforcement ratios within the first few sessions of each new condition and matched their relative rate of foraging time to relative rate of resources."[2] They paid attention. They counted. They altered their behavior logically. The buggers were every bit as clever as the animals of myth and legend. Perhaps more so.

Such basic science provides important clues about the kinds of things people must pay attention to when managing predators. For a carnivore, life is a game of rolling dice for food while minimizing risk, but it is 24/7, with no opportunity to move away from the table. The only way to win is to pay very close attention. People had to pay attention, too, and there was one more important level of complexity.

Lynne's background and animal-loving tendencies sometimes separated her from scientific convention. To the consternation of her traditionally trained major professor, she assigned individual names to her study subjects. "Scientists are not supposed to do that. It could inject bias; you'd expect an animal would act like its name,"

he cautioned. It would be too tempting to interpret, for example, that a coyote called "Softy" was responding more timidly than "Growly." Luckily, Lynne ignored him, and the blinders of ostensible objectivity didn't obscure her vision.

"Red was sort of reddish," Lynne said. (She was not always imaginative when she named her coyotes.) "His mate was Sub." Short for *subordinate*, Sub had a modus operandi of being "cute, charming, gentle and nonconfrontational." She looked the part, too, with big, fluffy puppy paws. No matter who or what approached her, she was submissive. Far from being sentimental himself, Red would bully her incessantly. He bullied Lynne, too. If her foot-pedal boxes remained in his pen a moment too long after a trial, he'd destroy them. How'd she know when it was too long? When he ate the lid.

Feisty had attitude. "Nothing fazed her," Lynne observed. Feisty was astonishingly clever too, which made her a pain to work with; she would learn readily, but in her own way. Most coyotes were easily trained to stomp on the food pedals, but Feisty would head butt the feeder to obtain the reward. She figured out how to unscrew devices from their anchors and run off with them. She was as different from Sub as Sub was from Red.

Dom was "a bit of a melon," as Lynne described him. He typically took longer to figure things out. He insisted on employing his nose, stabbing at the pedals like a woodpecker.

Matey was the representative Piglet of the ersatz Hundred Acre Wood. He was nervous and diminutive, afraid of everything. Most coyotes, ravenous, would eventually learn to overcome great fears and worries in order to obtain another morsel. Matey could not, however, be coaxed by great piles of the most attractive slop. If people were around, he wouldn't notice food at all. He didn't like entering tight spaces; he absolutely refused to go through any door. He didn't maximize the gathering of food, but rather minimized the risk of searching for it.

An apt appellation, Chewy was a rather obstreperous and intolerant animal. Chewy lovingly chewed the antenna off of her mate's GPS collar. She was hell bent on chewing on—not in a nice way—the animals in neighboring pens too. Her propensities were animated and exciting, but simultaneously dull. She was by far the most predictable of the coyotes—which also made her different. She had things she liked to do, but insisted on doing them the same way every time. If there was a task to perform, such as approaching and moving through a door in her pen, it would be a Groundhog Day event. She'd walk up to it from the same angle every time, moving through as if on a guided track.

The more Lynne interacted with her coyotes, the more she saw recognizable strategies in her study subjects' individual approaches to life. An old pair, Bob and Mrs. Bob, were like a bickering, long-married couple. To Lynne, it wasn't that she assigned or attributed human characteristics to the animals, in the anathema known as anthropomorphizing, but that the coyotes chose to be who they were. "Mrs. Bob wore the pants in the family. She'd make this hilarious 'yuck yuck' noise," Lynne said. Old Bob, on the other hand, was nervous and afraid of everything. His greatest solace in life was to consider food and lethargy as a means to a calmer and more comfortable end. He was by far the fattest of the lot. Bob was Winnie the Pooh to Matey's Piglet, or Missy's Tigger, or Feisty's wise old Owl.

The phenomenon Lynne was embracing was something that scientists had forced themselves to forget. After months of observing individual coyotes, Lynne concluded that her animals took different paths to overcome obstacles. They were individuals. It was a fresh perspective because most biologists ignore variability as noise and not as the important effect. Biologists create a Frankenstein monster by stitching their many behaviors into a single average. But is there such thing as an average coyote, bear, cougar, or wolf? Or human?

Thus, a single, one-size-fits-all solution to the predator paradox is not possible.

◗ ◗ ◗

Animal-care technician, graduate student, and salt-of-the-earth guy Patrick Darrow was tempted to kick and destroy the box of electronics on which the success of his graduate career was dependent. He volunteered, became a technician, rose to the dubious rank of graduate student, and was considering returning to the farm. A frustrating inside joke about scientific papers is that their "methods" sections are usually a few simple paragraphs. Life is edited down and condensed for clarity, leaving out the excitement. Years of toil, late nights, and frustration become, "We exposed coyotes to three different types of stimuli each week." For Patrick, both coyotes and electronics were complicated and prone to loose connections. The paper he would publish would simply assert that testing "was conducted from 17 July to 31 August" but would omit the meals he missed and the juggling, begging, and praying he had to do to get everything to work just right while he kept up with his wife and kids.[3]

Still, much of the initial groundwork had already been done in his quest to frighten predators away from food resources. Other scientists had measured coyote, wolf, and bear responses to fladry and other stimuli. Studies on the Critter Gitter were limited to one little device with one type of sound. The device Patrick wanted to test—the latest programmable improvement to the Radio Activated Guard—was more complicated and clever. It employed a variety of loud noises and lights, as well as motion sensors, to increase the scariness of the stimuli.

The research grew out of some conversations with Lynne but also from Patrick's own past. Growing up around cows, cats, and dogs on the farm, he knew that animals' responses were not always predictable. He'd even raised a coyote pup earlier in his career as a technician at the Predator Research Facility. He had been instructed to frolic, play, and tame it. The result from treating a young coyote like a golden retriever, however, was far from successful. Indeed, the effort backfired.

The coyote grew up confident, but it also grew to see Patrick as an unworthy alpha male, needing to be kicked out of the territory so that a new coyote could take over. The situation became dangerous. Patrick could expertly handle, bare-handed, any other coyote at the facility, but the coyote named Solo he could not. Solo gave every indication that he would fight Patrick to the death.

Working at the facility for years, Patrick had a unique and extended familiarity with the coyotes there. It was obvious to him that some of the coyotes were bold and dominant while others were shy and secretive. It wasn't that one coyote had a gestalt as much as all of them together formed one, a whole of many diverse elements in the complexity that described coyotes. His observations, however, were still just anecdotes, and even years of stories did not equal *data*. The idea of individual variation—personality—in mammalian predators required rigorous and repeatable investigation.

The idea and acceptance of animal personality is important because individual animals, and not conglomerated averages, are what come into conflict with people. Some bears remain in the woods eating nuts and berries while others descend into towns to search for food. Some wolves pass cattle on their way to kill elk. Some coyotes feast on rabbits and rodents while others are tempted toward lambs. Whether or not an animal ends up in a campground or pasture is dependent on the individual animal's inclinations. But there was another facet to these considerations: Was the likelihood of a predator being deterred from visiting or attacking dependent on some measurable aspect of its personality? A bold coyote like Red showed a propensity to take risks and investigate something new and potentially dangerous, while a shy one like Matey would give in quickly to fears. Patrick wanted to understand the continuum of bold and shy personalities in his population of coyotes.

If an animal was aggressive and dominant, would it be more likely to kill livestock or attack people? And, frustratingly, could it be that the very nature that makes it a problem animal also makes it one of the most difficult to repel? What frightens bold animals? Clearly, we'd have to know something about who we were trying to frighten away if we were to design more effective repellents.

Patrick gathered a group of coyotes and programmed his movement-activated frightening device to fire its lights and sounds when the coyotes approached a ration of what he wryly called in his report "processed pork product" (hot dogs to you and me). The little black box looked like a Secret Service suitcase, but it had a strobe light on top and a small grille protecting an internal speaker. A cord led to the motion sensor, which Patrick mounted on a fence above the hot dogs. Trials required Patrick to stay at the facility until dark, after everyone had left, so there would be no disturbances. Alone, he plugged everything in, including a video camera to record coyote behaviors and a data logger to record device activations. As in most research, after the hurrying, it was time to wait.

In the end, Patrick observed distinct types of coyote personalities as the animals responded to the device. To his surprise, the observed behavior did not reflect a familiar bell-shaped curve from one extreme to the other, with a continuum of bold to shy and most clumping around a middle average. The coyotes actually sorted themselves into groups.

There was a skittish and wary group of eight coyotes that the device terrified. They gave up trying to approach and never ate the hot dogs. Three other coyotes were the opposite, activating the device more than 110 times each and eating the treats in the first nights. They simply did not care. That was bold. But the group that was the most interesting was composed of four coyotes that were more than shy and less than bold. Initially, they were frightened by the device and ran like the shy coyotes, but then something peculiar and different happened. They tried again and ran. Then again and again. Eventually, they forced themselves to learn the limits of the disruptive stimulus, that the lights and sounds of Patrick's device were harmless. They habituated and ate the hot dogs with relish.

So it is clear that there are differences between individual animals. What about the differences between species? Are there some generalizations that we can make? Are things like fladry or RAG boxes scary and effective for some species, but completely ignored and ineffective for others? This was the question we unintentionally tackled by distributing free meals in the form of road-killed deer while testing fladry for wolves in Wisconsin.

We identified six wolf packs in the flats and forests south of Spooner, Wisconsin. Within each pack's territory, we installed three plots and delineated them with nylon ropes to form a teardrop-shaped section of forest, more or less ten meters in circumference. Kerry Martin, the technician working on the project, then had the unique honor of dragging road-killed deer into the center of each plot over the course of the study.[4]

To gather information about what predators visited and how much meat was consumed, Kerry visited plots at two- to three-day intervals, weighing carcasses and checking for predator sign. It was immediately obvious that both wolves and bears were using the area and enjoying the free food. After a couple weeks of baiting, treatments were applied: a Movement Activated Guard (the RAG with a motion detector instead of a radio), fladry, and a control that had no frightening device.

As the study progressed, feeding not only continued but increased on unprotected plots. The fladry failed, too; carcasses were still consumed after the flagging was installed. No statistical difference was detectable between fladry and the control.

Why did the fladry fail? The plots were indeed placed in the middle of wolf territories. The wolves in Musiani's work clearly showed that they should have been afraid of the fladry. Such a failure to prevent intrusions was puzzling.

Technology once again came to the rescue when we reviewed the surveillance video at each site. The answer emerged slowly, lumbering along in grainy night-vision video recordings.

The experiment was ostensibly about wolves, but in actuality it wasn't. Indeed, the wolves were repelled and rarely visited the plots. On one stormy night, for example, a thin wolf approached the ropes that delineated the plot. Its eyes flickered in the infrared light as snowflakes whirled through the frame. It approached slowly, cautiously, and then disappeared. Hours passed before it returned. The wolf moved closer again, excruciatingly slowly to a human observer. It sniffed at the rope. It bounded away.

In other video, however, the real interlopers appeared: black bears. In contrast with the wolves, the bears loped over and through the ropes and flags without pause. Fladry, and the smell and activities of humans—anathema to wolves—are irrelevant white noise to bears. It took Kerry hours to drag in a carcass, while it took a bear seconds to pick it up and walk away with it, nimbly stepping out of the plot. Quite unlike wolves, bears had little worry or concern. They stepped on the ropes, sniffed around carcasses, and lazily ate their meals. One bear, intensely curious, disrespectfully swatted the observation camera from the tree. We were left with hours of observation of a spot on the forest floor.

The MAG was different. Watching a supremely confident bear lope into the corral was entertaining. But watching the first flash of a MAG transmogrify a 200-pound bruin from the epitome of insouciance into the quintessence of hysteria in a millisecond was hilarious. Bears strolled up, then leaped and bounded away, their full, rounded butts jiggling as they galloped off the screen. The MAG device reduced consumption by 68 percent during the treatment period, even while consumption at the other sites increased.

Species do differ dramatically. Wary critters such as coyotes and wolves will be dissuaded by a passive virtual barrier like fladry. Species such as bears, which are curious and confident, require a different approach. Cougars, still untested, are probably somewhere in between. The species-specific aspect of the predator paradox is another indicator that, while effective nonlethal methods for preventing predation exist, there is no one-size-fits-all solution.

Knowledge of differences between species will help us devise and apply more selective methods for many problems at hand, but noting differences within species also provides potential inroads for research. Not only do individual animals behave differently, as Lynne's named coyotes did, but they have a way of creating a culture wherein individual behaviors are policed, like Alex Mettler's guard coyotes. Thus the presence and pressure of peers deserve our attention too.

Are predators models for humans or are humans models for predators? Were Lynne's coyotes doing calculations similar to hers? That is, Lynne had to balance the benefits of living in a foreign country with the perils of working at its Predator Research Facility. One could be bitten. There was the time spent on animal care, or the time when she couldn't access her subjects because another student was doing behavioral observations and needed to restrict access to the facility. She depended on her lab mates and the facility staff while competing with them for time and resources. There was something deeply personal in her research questions as they addressed the nature of her subjects' intelligence and sociality. For predators, two competing motivations led to, or prevented, depredations on livestock: hunger for food and aversion to risk. Coyotes, like humans, had choices to make, and there was great intellectual allure in understanding how they optimized their paths through life.

Lynne's next experiment addressed ideas of dominance and

deception, an effort related to the work Alex Mettler had begun with fladry. Lynne built on the previous work, delving deeper into additional aspects of sociality and learning. Did coyotes exchange information in much the same way that rumors spread through the College of Natural Resources building when there was a pile of bagels in the lobby? There wasn't only one answer to that question. Context and quantity changed the calculations. With the abundance of free treats in the bagel scenario, information spread rapidly. When there wasn't enough to share, a student's strategy was different. A graduate student is a hungry beast. Mark Twain's description of the coyote reminds me of my own days in graduate school: "A living, breathing allegory of Want. He is always hungry. He is always poor."[5] When there is only one treat left, it is almost certainly eaten by its discoverer.

Lynne sorted out eight coyote pairs and began to play hide and seek games with their food, but she included the complication of social context.[6] The experiment was first about each animal's foraging efficiency and its ability to track food locations. The social twist was examining how subordinate and dominant animals interacted when only one had information.

For the experiment, Lynne devised a foot-long tube feeder that was open on one end and capped on the other. The capped end held food that was inaccessible, so it could serve as an olfactory control. The open side could be stuffed with food that a coyote could shake out. Each tube had the smell, but only one had a reward stuffed into the accessible side.

She positioned the feeders in an arc that spanned the test area, about ninety yards from a smaller holding area. In the holding area, the coyotes were blind to the experimental conditions being set for them. Lynne divided the pen so that the feeders were each put into different blocks that were twice as close to each other within quadrants (about seven yards apart) versus between quadrants (fourteen yards apart).

The first experiments involved locking the dominant animal in the holding area and having only the subordinate coyotes search for food at the feeders. After an animal found the treats and ate, it was herded back into the holding area. The trial was repeated, but the food was always in the same place the second time. The coyotes learned quickly, of course, and most played the game five or six times before consistently returning to the correct feeder. The worst of the "melons," in Lynne's parlance, needed thirteen trials before getting a perfect score.

In the second part of the experiment, it was a dominant coyote's turn. The conditions were similar, but with a crucial difference: in a dominant animal's second search, food was never in the same place as it was in the first trial. The dominant was guessing where the food was in both trials, while the subordinate knew where it was the second time.

The fun part was running the two animals together when the subordinate knew where the food was, but the dominant didn't. It was like real life, where one individual had information and the other had power.

Given the dynamics of the coyote dyad, the subordinate animal was presented with a new puzzle in the second trial: If it ran right to the correct feeder, the dominant would follow and immediately displace them from the food. If it didn't bother trying, it would not even get a bite. Would a subordinate coyote use "reverse psychology" and go to the wrong feeder to bluff the dominant one?

Ultimately, when the pair was released simultaneously, the subordinate did not run right at the food. Neither did it try a bluff or a ploy. Isaac Asimov said, "The most exciting phrase to hear in science, the one that heralds new discoveries, is not 'Eureka!' ('I found it!') but rather 'Hmm . . . that's funny.'"[7] Such was the moment of understanding for Lynne and her colleagues.

In Shakespeare, Hamlet had the unfortunate dilemma of having an unreliable source tell him that his uncle, the current king, had killed his father by pouring poison in his ear. Hamlet feared rushing in with treasonous accusations, so he approached the question indirectly using his famous play within the play, having minstrels test the king by acting out Hamlet's hypothesis. He set up the king and then watched.

In the coyote opera, subordinate coyotes also approached the puzzle indirectly. They did indeed run toward the correct location—but then stopped short. They repeatedly chose the correct quadrant right out of the chute, but did not follow through to the food and risk conflict with the dominant animal. They knew and positioned themselves where they could take advantage if the opportunity presented itself, but they decidedly gave in to their fear and yielded to the dominant animal's search. They stopped short of dashing to the right feeder until they saw what the dominant would do.[8]

In a result that is anathema to an academic, the observed behavior meant that the power of social hierarchy and the fear of repercussions trumped knowledge. It meant that predators had to live with each other and make decisions based on much more complex considerations than merely the emptiness of their stomachs.

For those of us seeking to resolve conflicts between ourselves and hungry carnivores, however, it was actually good news. Here was a hint that different approaches could be effective. It wasn't only a dead coyote that didn't eat but also a frightened or intimidated one. It meant that subtle but clever force magnifiers could be developed that would amplify the effectiveness of tools and techniques. Lethal techniques remove animals but also have the consequence of throwing social units, territories, allies, and enemies into disarray. From the work of Mettler, Gilbert-Norton, and others, however, it is clear that elements of sociality—essentially peer pressure—could be used to help us achieve our goals.

CHAPTER 7

OF SPIKED DOUGHNUTS AND TURBO-CHARGED FLAGGING

Testing Aversive Stimuli

Kari Signor wasn't much taller than the plastic bins that she bolted to a tree and filled with doughnuts. Her Carhartts were smeared with icing and spilled latte, their cargo pockets filled with D batteries. She measured out the pastries she had sweet-talked from the Moab grocer then mixed in a precise amount of the active compound, thiabendazole (TBZ). The swirl of SpongeBob SquarePants birthday cake lost its chance to hold seven candles for its intended audience, but it was going to make a black bear very happy, at least for a while.[1]

Kari's technician, Dustin Ranglack, stepped lightly over a polygon of barbed wire that surrounded the barrel of cake and doughnuts. The barbs were clever catchers of bear hair for genetic analysis. The blonde-haired, blue-eyed, neat, and impeccably wholesome native Utahan contrasted in countenance and demeanor with his wild-haired graduate student boss. He moved from barb to barb, removing hairs and putting them into small sample envelopes, labeling each with its date and location then filing it for its trip to the lab. Firing up a lighter, he waved a flame beneath each barb, destroying any remnant DNA that could corrupt future samples. The hair collection done, Dustin unbolted the motion-activated camera from its aspen. A quick insertion of a data card and a few button presses and they had the data. He checked the batteries and returned the camera to its mount, making certain it was properly aimed at the trash bin.

Kari, filling the plastic can with cake and TBZ, was trying to instill something called *conditioned taste aversion*, or CTA, in the bears. TBZ, a readily available veterinary compound normally used as a deworming medicine, was considered tasteless and easily hidden in foodstuffs. Kari wasn't worried about parasitic worms in the bear population, but she was interested in one of the compound's particular side effects: it caused roll-on-the-ground nausea in animals that consumed enough of it.

Kari garnished the recipe by spraying a solution of camphor oil onto the mix of cakes and doughnuts. The camphor, presumably odiferous and foreign to a bear in the woods, was to be a unique signal, a smell unlike anything they had detected before. If she could get CTA to work, the smell of camphor would cause illness. Then the normally innocuous chemical would be transformed into an effective repellent. Using such a repellent could keep conditioned bears out of campgrounds, cars, and cabins from Yosemite to the Adirondacks.

The phenomenon of CTA has been thoroughly studied by psychologists since the pioneering work of John Garcia in the 1950s.[2] Garcia would flavor water and then make mice dreadfully ill with either radiation or a chemical, such as lithium chloride. The mice's minds paired the feeling of illness with the novel flavors they had recently consumed. They would then abhor the flavors. Spurred on by Garcia's groundbreaking results and clever experiments, fellow psychologists expanded on the research, demonstrating the strength and universality of CTA in a myriad of animals.

The step was made from mice to coyotes and wolves, and as early as the 1970s psychologists thought they had stumbled upon the best solution to predation problems.[3] Unfortunately, to the chagrin of many, capabilities of wildlife biologists are still mired where the psychologists' were decades ago.[4] Essentially, some psychologists championed CTA as a panacea, but wildlife biologists could not replicate the effects in the field and at a scale meaningful to managers. There were intense frustrations on both sides of the issue and the controversy grew. Each side accused the other of either poor science or blind advocacy.[5] Frustrations of early proponents exist still, as do rambling indictments of conspiracy by the wildlife biologist elite.[6] Rather than continue to be confused by historic arguments, Kari decided to collect data.

In the context of the laboratory, few behavioral phenomena have been explored as thoroughly as CTA. Every animal, from honeybees to ravens to rats, has circuitry deep within the primitive base of its brain—an unconscious connection with the gut. The neurons respond when a particular taste is paired with sickness. The reflex evolved in early animals and the biological significance is obvious: having the ability to resist poisons even before developing the ability for conscious reasoning was certainly an advantage for prototypical beasts. Psychologists hijack the circuitry when they play games with CTA, pairing a normally innocuous flavor with a cause of gastrointestinal malaise. Suddenly, the waft of an irrelevant odor is transformed into a salient one that represents intense physical discomfort. After conditioning, an animal becomes overwhelmingly queasy with only a sniff.

It works on humans as well as mice.[7] A personal example comes to mind: I was young and my family and I were traveling to visit relatives. Pinched for time and resources, my mother had prepared canned spaghetti. I had never eaten Chef Boyardee before. By chance, and likely due to my exposure to novel pathogens while traveling, I felt the effect of gut-bending stomach flu the next day. For years afterwards, if someone opened a can of the brand, or I tasted a similarly flavored sauce, my cheeks would pucker and my stomach would turn. The idea of even getting near the sauce, much less consuming it, remains—decades later—utterly repulsive to me. Of no small consequence is the fact that once is enough with CTA: getting sick on tequila the first time you drink it will do. With elusive and secretive predators, such one-trial yet long-lasting learning is a Holy Grail phenomenon.

The American black bear is becoming America's heftiest and most ubiquitous pest, responsible for almost four thousand kills and about $769,000 in livestock damage annually. The bears are the bane of bird-feeders, campers, and Stephen Colbert alike, and conflicts with them are growing rapidly. Black bears' insatiable appetites, termed *hyperphagia*, drive them to search for food and eat almost constantly. *Walking stomachs*, some biologists call them. The bears pay attention to little else in the spring, and when they find a food source they remember it. Bears return year after year, mothers teaching cubs where the good pickings are. They are good learners.

Some black bears have even learned to specialize in certain car models. Stewart Breck and his team with the National Wildlife Research Center worked with managers at Yosemite National Park to identify trends in bear damage to vehicles.[8] The results of their analyses were striking—and amusing. Would the prissy and easily accessible soft-topped sports cars, redolent of animal leather, be prone to damage?

Actually, no. Bears avoided the manicured machines. Would sports cars be littered with cereal, chips, and other snacks? No, they'd be pampered and clean. Who entertains with food on long road trips? Who trucks around kids who leave smears of sweet smelling treats on the seats and drop crumbs into every crevice? Parents. What do they drive? Minivans. In Breck's study, gleaning data from 908 vehicles that bears broke into from 2001 through 2007, more than one-quarter of the break-ins involved minivans (1.7 percent for sports cars). In the peak year, 29 percent of the break-ins involved minivans—a rate statistically higher than expected given the number of minivans that were driven into the park.

Kari Signor wanted to know if CTA could be used to take human's scraps, whether in minivans or vacation cabins, off of bear menus by transforming them into something unpalatable. It had been done successfully before. Bears that were breaking into trailers at a military reservation ceased the behavior when the military rations—meals ready to eat—were similarly spiked.[9] But such successes usually occurred in situations where biologists could see and size up an animal, then deliver dosages accurately and individually. Kari didn't know if treating food piles in campgrounds would work.[10]

Working on public land in the La Sal Mountains of southeast

Utah, Kari tried to hide her sites so that people would not van-dalize them or, God forbid, eat the doughnuts. She had to spread all twenty-four sites (twelve control and twelve treated with TBZ) across the landscape in places that weren't necessarily the most convenient for her to monitor. This took tons of driving, including frequent trips down the hill to gather bait from the bakery section of the Moab grocery market.

There were long nights of data analysis, when she and her tech-nician scanned through videos, counting bear visits and recording time stamps in a spreadsheet. The videos provided exciting footage of bears. Kari had her own private nature show. In one sequence, three cubs—like little stuffed animals—frolicked in and out of a bin, their tiny feet grasping the rim to keep them from falling in. Elk, and even a cougar, walked through the frames.

On one of the videos she saw a man rummaging in a blue plas-tic bin. He couldn't steal it, because the hex bolts that attached the garbage can to the tree could be detached only with a half-inch socket. In the short sequence of his visit, the man straddled the barbed wire bear-hair collector and stretched to look into the can. The feat took some skill because his blue jeans and ratty gray underwear—their tattered fabric breaking away from the waist-band—had been slipped down around his knees. The man wore a tree-camo jacket and a ball cap turned backward. He stumbled only slightly, the round, white moon of his buttocks panning in front of the camera. It was more funny than unnerving, but Kari concluded that it was definitely people who were most unpredictable and dif-ficult to manage.

Kari anxiously scanned through the spreadsheet, which featured almost as many colors as the Excel palette would allow—a fresh shade for every different data type in rows and columns, looking like a rainbow across the screen. She noted that more bears had returned to the treatment sites than to the controls—exactly the opposite of her hypothesis. TBZ did not seem to be packing the Sunday morning post-binge misery into the doughnuts that it had promised. Kari's graduate career and the ignominy of negative results flashed on the Mac before her. TBZ had worked for other scientists, why wasn't it working for her?

After spending two summers on fieldwork, placing pounds of pastries and analyzing DNA gleaned from seventy-nine hair samples, Kari was left with results that fell far short of identifying a magic bullet or arrow, or even pea-shooter. Metrics of bear behavior at control and treatment sites were similar during baseline and treatment periods, but bear visits actually increased at treated sites following application of TBZ and camphor. During the baseline phase, Kari collected hair from six different individual bears at control sites and ten different bears at treatment sites. Following treatment, most revisits were to sites treated with TBZ and camphor (nine revisits), rather than to the control sites (three revisits). Was the odor of camphor actually acting as a positive reinforcer? (Smell camphor: get food.) The results were frustrating.

Did the results mean that CTA doesn't work? Did they mean there is a conspiracy by modern wildlife managers against using it? No, on both accounts. A plethora of evidence on so many species over so many years demonstrates the strength of the effect. CTA is as real as the queasiness in my gut when I smell canned spaghetti and sauce, but translating from lab to free-roaming animals is not easy or automatic. I have been sick many times, but I rarely form an aversion to what I ate the night before. With CTA, the consequence does not have to follow ingestion swiftly, but the taste must stand out and be particularly salient. The context and conditions have to be right. It's not that there is a conspiracy,[11] but rather wildlife biologists haven't been clever enough to make CTA work for predators, except in limited situations.[12]

So it goes in coexisting with wandering predators. It is not a simple, linear, or one-step proposition. It will take a series of experiments, with more failures than successes, until an army of possibilities is available. It will require people from wide-ranging backgrounds attempting different approaches, some from right field, some from left, some from little towns in Idaho, or from Bristol in the south of England. Living with predators will take work and persistence.

When an ambition is accomplished easily, one rarely learns,

much less grows. Moments of failure are what determine success; nothing teaches like a setback, if one has the will to proceed. We humans are apex predators, too, and if we are to collaborate with the wild ones around us, we have to be equally diligent about staying the course. When wolves are scared away from a potential food source by an electronic guard, they don't give up. Because so much is at stake, they alter their tactics and attempt to adapt. In our relationship with these predators there is much at stake for us as well, and we ought to follow in their footsteps.

In the mid-1920s, Ivan Pavlov famously approached a dog with a bell and meat powder in experiments describing a phenomenon that would become known as *classical conditioning*. Several years later, Burrhus Frederic Skinner favored a box with a lever and a rat in his experiments. In contrast to Pavlov's classical conditioning view, Skinner looked at the world through an *operant conditioning* lens. In operant mode, also known as trial-and-error learning, the animal chooses a line of behaviors based on positive rewards or negative outcomes. Behaviors are shaped more than made.

But animals did other things that seemed to have nothing to do with such positive or negative motivators. In the 1940s and '50s, ethologist powerhouses including Konrad Lorenz and Niko Tinbergen concluded that an animal's behavior was ultimately the result of its genetic mapping and innate mechanisms. They cited nesting geese as proof. If an egg rolls out from a nest, a graylag goose will retrieve it by walking backwards and side to side, tucking its chin and scooping the egg back in. Comically, even if a person removes the egg in the middle of the behavior, the bird will continue to scoop and push at air until it has returned to the nest. The series of movements is triggered like a reflex, but the response is complex, like dancing instead of kicking after a tap on the patellar tendon.

Scientists and their intellectual progeny wanted to understand behavior, but because the framework was different for each scientific camp's schema, the interpretations and explanations for behaviors varied widely. Various scientists interested in animal behavior pledged allegiance to one school or the other. They eventually separated themselves with a schism as wide as the Atlantic.

It wasn't until the 1970s and '80s that scientists accepted the notion that various approaches had their uses. But the divisive battles had set the stage for a great deal of confusion regarding "correct" methods for altering the behaviors of animals.

Sometimes the genetics of a species is the most important determinant. Other times natural variability—the engine of evolution—throws us a curve. When it is predatory behavior that we want to change, however, a failed approach can be devastating and dangerous.

Kari Signor's application of CTA can be understood under the light of the theorists. When Pavlov's dog smelled the meat powder, it instinctively salivated—the innate, instinctual response that interested Lorenz. The next layer in conditioning was the sound of a bell—the ringing that until that point was meaningless to the dog. By repeatedly pairing the bell sound with the arrival of the food, however, it became *the* signal to eat, as relevant as the smell of the meat itself. Kari's pairing was similar to Pavlov's, but had a repulsive consequence rather than an attractive one. TBZ caused sickness, and the smell of camphor signaled it. Therefore, camphor should eventually have repelled the bears, if it was done right.

But she didn't do something right, and we still don't know what it was.

Like the wolves that altered their approach when they encountered the wails of the first Radio Activated Guard, Kari regrouped and tried to flank the problem, circling the hill and trying from a different angle. She backtracked to examine her initial assumptions.

If it is only food that motivates bears, and they act as automatons—stimulus-response, or in the case of food, no stimulus-no response—then taking away a food source should result in no bears. This Kari did, again wandering through the La Sal mountains and filling cans with doughnuts and creamy cakes.[13]

She established twenty-two experimental sites. After a four-week baseline period, she divided the sites into control and treatment pairs. Controls continued to be baited during the summer treatment period. Treatment bins were cleaned and left empty.

As expected, the number and duration of bear visits declined after food was removed from the treatment sites. Bears came only every five days, versus every day and a half where food remained. The bears that did visit the sites without food lumbered around, but they did not dive into the empty bins. The experiment was a success, but there was a catch, a discrepancy that muddled the clarity of results.

Bears reduced their visits to treatment sites, but did not abandon them. They had not received a reward in weeks, but still they came. Indeed, the difference in activity that Kari measured between control and treatment was not because all bears had stopped coming. Using the genetic analysis to identify individuals, she could tell that the difference was because new bears stopped visiting. The ones that had found food previously continued their incursions. Having found food only once or twice, they searched and sampled the site for weeks later.

Bears learn and remember well. Cabin owners and campers should remember this: people have to leave food out only once. It could be a forgotten bag of pet food on the porch or bits of meat on the grill. If a bear finds the food and eats, then stopping the bear from returning is far more difficult than just cleaning up the next time.

Another real-world example that has trapped biologists and laypeople alike is essentially an effect of poor aim: a swing and a miss when applying aversive stimuli. Consider the act of shooting a bear with a rubber bullet to scare it away from a campground. It runs away. We feel happy that we did something, but what exactly did we do? Did we condition the bear away from the campground?

At the moment a biologist arrives, the bear is surrounded by a plethora of stimuli: trees, grass, and landscape. Those are all neutral. Even a truck pulling up initially means nothing to the lumbering brute. Soon after the truck slows and parks, however, the bear hears the pop of the weapon and feels the sting of a round on its rump. A few repetitions of this and a connection will form. Indeed, a bear in these circumstances usually does become conditioned. But to what?

The same old trees are there, as are the grass and rocks and a myriad of signals that had never caused a stinging rump before. The bear's internal computer searches for a cause to link with the effect, something new to pair the negative stimulus with. Conditioning is precise, not general. The bear seeks something that stands out, like the smoke-belching fish and game department truck. Signal: truck. Stimulus: sting of rubber bullet. Our bear conditions against the truck. Sometimes aversive conditioning works like we want it to and sometimes it doesn't.[14] A danger of misapplied aversive conditioning is that we all too often teach the animals to become more secretive and clever, which perhaps is more of a problem.

Aversive conditioning is an alluring weapon. We hope for guard wolves and guard coyotes, bears and cougars that avoid areas or livestock forever. With disruptive stimuli, animals react in ways that protect a resource, but predators take conditioning with them.

The challenge with aversive conditioning is not only provoking the aversion, but actually linking that conditioning to the precise behavior we are trying to reduce. For predators, the internal dialogue of death is a complicated conversation. With aversive conditioning, we are trying to add a third voice into an adaptive dialogue, but we have only a rudimentary knowledge of the language.

Ted Turner was doing his part for the conservation of predators and natural ecosystems, although he was not there to guide the particulars and had little familiarity with the details. Those were left to the biologists, like Val Asher.

Val would have been perfectly cast as the resourceful, confident, borderline-truculent heroine in a dusty western. She had dark eyes and wavy brown hair, but was so tough and scrappy that you almost forgot how pretty she was. I could not imagine that she'd ever appear in a dainty dress, much less petticoats. A long-time wolf trapper, Val played the part accurately.

Val dragged a raw calf hide into a pen and threw it over a stuffed red doggy back-pack that bulged with cables and a small antenna.

Three young wolves paced in the far corner of the pen, stopping frequently to watch her. Employees of the Turner Endangered Species Fund, including Val, had reconstructed the pen on the edge of a soft meadow on the Flying D Ranch not far from Bozeman, Montana. The pen's panels had originally held the pack of wolves that were released in Yellowstone's Lamar Valley.

Val dropped her pack and removed a radio collar from it. Attached to the collar slightly above the transmitter was a cheaper plastic box. It had two metal probes that protruded through the leather of the collar. A little diode, like a naked Christmas tree light, was strung between the inch-long blunt-tipped spikes. Val approached the hide again, stooped down, and swung the collar over it slowly. It made no sound, but the diode glowed brightly, then dimmed as she backed away. The light indicated that touching the probes would be painful when it was lit. When she approached the hide, electronics hidden beneath, the collar charged the probes, lit the light. When she retreated, it calmed.

The Sheep Mountain Boys, as she called the wolves, were three young males who had gotten into trouble with cattle. After capture, they were more or less "dead wolves walking," and their immediate penance was to participate in an experiment on aversive conditioning. Living in the half-acre pen, they were given a stay of execution, and we hoped it would result in a full pardon.

The idea for the experiment drew upon big-box pet store technology. Dogs were trained with shock-collars in suburban homes everywhere, so it followed that if shock collars were put on wolves, and wolves were zapped when they approached a calf, they would learn that calves were not worth the trouble to kill and eat. By endowing cattle with something akin to electronic quills, the approach would teach wolves to avoid calves much as they avoid porcupines in favor of less painful prey, such as deer or elk. If the conditioning took, the Sheep Mountain Boys could live among the cattle that spread out over the landscape. Not only would they not eat the cattle in their territory, they'd prevent other wolves from entering and becoming a threat.

Val was nothing if not serious about wolves. She was definitely an advocate but also a pragmatist. First, the concept had to be demonstrated, tested scientifically. Working with living, thinking, and independently behaving animals made what should have been simple experiments challenging. Wild animals did not always perform as expected. The initial control trials had certainly gone humorously awry.

Part of the Flying D's mission was to promote a herd of bison, but as nature took its course, protecting the herd was not easy or assured. A few days earlier, a bison calf had been orphaned. The calf's long-term survival was doubtful. A solution was for the "dead bison walking" to meet the "dead wolves walking." The experiment provided an opportunity for the scientific team to demonstrate to the wolves that natural prey were fair game: bison was good to kill and consume. Later they'd be taught that domestic animals weren't.

Val shooed and cussed at the waist-high calf as she prodded it into the pen and secured the gate behind it. It was up to nature, red in tooth and claw, once she left the bison with the wolves. If the stuff of Bozeman pool-hall talk was accurate, the wolves would descend upon the helpless beast like famished demons, shredding it rapidly and thoroughly.

Instead, the wolves raised their heads and watched, curious, as the calf surveyed the pen. It ignored them and picked around through drying July vegetation. The three wolves swung downwind of the calf and approached slowly, but it seemed blissfully unaware of their intentions. The boldest of the boys, M195, moved ahead and led the pack with its head down and eyes focused like lasers. The wolf stepped lightly toward the baby bison. The calf raised its head too, observing the predator before it. It snorted. The wolf inched closer.

Val zoomed in with her spotting scope as the natural drama unfolded before her. The death had to be quick. According to the protocol, if the wolves toyed and tormented the bison or were sloppy in their killing, she and her colleagues would have to rush in and euthanize the animal, potentially complicating the experiment, but preventing unneeded suffering.

She focused on the scene in time to see the calf lower its head

like a Spanish *toro* and charge. The New World wolf froze, knowing nothing of *una buena faena*. The calf charged forward and
butted the predator broadside, which sent the confused canid tum-
bling down the hill. After a few rolls and a simper, M195 was up
again and scampering away from new emperor of the pen.

"Caesar," Val said, having given the bison calf its imperial appellation, "he sort of owns the pen now." It was not the vicious
predator, but rather the ostensibly vulnerable prey that was the alpha male in that pack, and the calf shamelessly exploited its dominance. On one occasion in the late summer heat, the wolves were
bedded under an aspen when Caesar approached. They rose defer-
entially and moved away so that the emperor could regurgitate his
cud in the coolness beneath the trees. Val, a field biologist through
and through, and one as distrustful of egg-headed academics as any
of the more practical sort, reminded me that university professors
have all the ideas and theories, but wolves don't read the books.

The Sheep Mountain Boys had to eat, and we wanted them to consider bison as the normal food, so eventually Caesar was euthanized
and the wolves enjoyed their meal. After the wolves were captured
and training collars fitted to their necks, Val began the next phase
of the experiment. She carefully put the transmitter under a cow-
hide to determine if the wolves would respond to the shock and
avoid the skin of a domestic cow. The system was designed to activate and shock if the wolves came within a meter of the transmitter.
As she waved the collar over the hide, Val saw by the glowing diode
that the test collar was activating. She retreated to her distant blind,
her spotting scope focused on the mat of hair.

The bold wolf, 195M, approached, and Val held her breath.
The animal swung downwind of the skin and sniffed the air around
it. He stepped cautiously toward the hide. Left paw, right paw, stop,
crouch. Distrustful, he retreated a few meters and sampled the air
again. Emboldened by the smell of flesh on hide, he approached
again until his nose was inches away. He could almost nip and taste
it. Val smiled when the wolf whipped upward and sprung back from
the mound of fur. The collar had surely activated. The wolf ran to

the far side of the pen and paced with his packmates, wary of the painful force. None of the wolves approached the hide again. Val nodded approvingly. Something was working.[15]

Bill Andelt, working at the Predator Research Facility in Utah in the 1990s, demonstrated how shock collars could be used to teach coyotes not to attack sheep.[16] An academic grandfather of Bill's, Sam Linhart, had previously proven how clever coyotes were many years before. Using shock collars, he taught a group of coyotes that white rabbits were okay to eat but that black rabbits packed a nasty sting.[17]

Electric shock is a standard aversive stimulus in the lab. The plethora of domestic dogs that wear training collars is additional proof of the strength of the concept. Andelt and Linhart's successes demonstrated that the techniques could be adapted for wild animals too. There was certainly enough previous theory and practice using training collars to put them on the Sheep Mountain Boys. By rapidly backing away and then avoiding the calf hide, the wolves in Val's experiment showed that they could be repelled too.

It was more reassuring when a domestic calf, wearing the transmitter in a backpack, was introduced into the pen. The results were boring, in that nothing happened, but also extraordinarily exciting precisely because nothing happened. The three wolves—predators that had fed on domestic livestock before, that had enjoyed killing rabbits in the pen and feasting on deer—never attacked the domestic calves that Val put in with them. Was their reluctance due to conditioning from the collar? It was impossible to prove in the one experiment, especially after seeing how they had reacted to Caesar. Also, there were only three wolves. Knowing what we know about animal personality and behavior, could strong conclusions be made about a wide-scale application of the technique? No. Other scientists would have to adapt it to a practical field application.

Jason Hawley, a student of Tom Gehring's at Central Michigan University, took up the challenge. He was able to apply the technique to free-ranging wolves, but he also had the advantage of hindsight. Our work at the Flying D taught us about various unforeseen logistical hurdles, the most significant of which was that training collars were not meant to be worn full time. The probes, if left on too long, irritated and abraded the wolves' necks.

If Jason was going to train free ranging wolves, he had to do something to make the collars fit well without injuring the wolves. He found an ally at the Wisconsin Department of Natural Resources in a gray-bearded field biologist named Ron Schultz. Ron was also actively trying to find ways to relieve the pressure of people on wolf populations of Wisconsin. He had been busy filing, brushing, and playing with springing probes so that they would keep good contact but not erode and damage skin and fur. After crafting several iterations, Jason latched onto the best designs and headed into the field.[18]

His study design, as with the best studies, was simple. He first trapped and radio-collared ten wolves. Half wore transmitters only, and the other half had transmitter-activated shock collars too. Thus, he had five control and five experimental wolves that he could monitor. He created five bait stations at forest trail intersections in the deciduous woods of the Wisconsin countryside. Each site had an inner shock zone with a thirty-meter radius, activated by a transmitter at its center. Similar to the monitor that Rick Williamson used to record wolf visits to RAG boxes in Idaho, Jason's could detect when wolves approached within seventy-five meters of road-killed deer carcasses at the center of the experimental zone, and when they came close enough to eat.

As the experiment continued, Jason searched through the data, the ones and zeros of wolf presence and absence at the sites. To boil the summer down to a sentence, Jason showed that shock-collared wolves spent less time and made fewer visits to the bait sites than the control animals.[19] It was a proof of concept, but more significantly, it had been done under field conditions.

One definition of good research is that it provides more than a *yes* or *no* answer to the hypothesis. The answer to *why* is also important and usually requires revisiting data and plodding through different possibilities. Sometimes a little extra effort pays off. For example, I had watched hours of surveillance videos of Kerry Martin's study plots in Wisconsin, where we had compared fladry to a Movement Activated Guard. The bears were all very amusing, but one video in particular captured my attention. It was a stormy evening and snow flew over the carcass in the middle of the frame. The flakes flashed in the infrared spotlight like hazy stars shooting across the screen. Across the plot, just outside of the roped border, two glowing eyes appeared.

Looking more closely at the video, I saw the face of a wolf emerge ghostlike from the darkness, eyes reflecting the infrared like a demon's. The wolf approached the rope that held the fladry, stopped, and then moved along its length. It jumped away and disappeared into the night. Using the time travel of fast-forward, I sped to the moment hours later when the animal reappeared. It approached again, cautiously stepping toward the ropes and flags that were bouncing and whipping in the midnight breeze. It thrust its muzzle forward and sniffed at the rope and then . . .

I paused the recording, then rewound and replayed it several times. It seemed so strange, but there it was in grainy black and white: the wolf had touched the fladry with its nose, sniffing first, but it also used its tongue and teeth. On the second probe, more confident, the wolf stretched out its neck, grabbed the nylon cord, and bit down. Its carnassial teeth sliced through the rope effortlessly. *Wolves*, I thought, *test with their mouths*. We could use that.

Fladry—based on the work of Marco Musiani, Elisabetta Visalberghi, and Alex Mettler—could keep canids at bay, at least for a little while. But they'd learn. They'd habituate. Could we use our knowledge about wolf behavior to improve on the technique? Nathan Lance proposed just that. He wanted to know if he could add a painful bite to the string of already scary flags. It would be a turbo-charged technique: as obvious as a billboard and charged like an electric fence. Scary at first, but when a wolf finally got the gumption to investigate, using its nose or tongue—two moist and extremely sensitive areas—the fladry would knock him off of his feet.

Nate was amiable and competent. He looked enough like a rancher's son to get along in Montana. He had a neatly trimmed beard, attractive blue eyes, and a way of smiling while he talked, which he did a lot. He tended to put those around him at ease.

He gathered up spools of electrified "turbo-fladry" and headed east, hoping to determine its effectiveness with wolves at Peggy Callahan's Wildlife Science Center. Using fifteen packs of wolves, Nate compared the effectiveness of electrified fladry to standard fladry for protecting a food resource. He selected five pens to receive fladry barriers, five to receive electrified fladry barriers, and five to serve as controls with no barrier. The experiment was simple. Wolves roamed large pens with a deer carcass in one corner, but with a sole string of fladry or turbo-fladry that blocked their access to it.[20]

In the control pens, wolves set upon the unprotected carcasses almost immediately. It generally took them five minutes to work up the nerve and move toward the dead deer. Where the novelty effect of new food was measured in minutes, the effect of fladry was measured in hours. It worked for a while, but because wolves were exposed to it constantly, they habituated quickly. The repellent effect of standard fladry lasted for one day. The effectiveness of electrified fladry, however, was measured in weeks. Wolves had constant opportunities to learn and devise ways to overcome the barrier, but they didn't.

Nate got to know his subjects well. Patrick Darrow's studies of the bold, persistent, and shy personality continuum influenced his observations, and he saw not only the average wolf pack but also the individual animals, including how and what they learned. He studied how they challenged the electrified fladry. After first learning of its shock, the wolves generally reduced their approaches during the two-week trial. Some wolves, however, tested the barrier frequently. One bold pack tried about eight hundred times to find a way to cross. Another two made around seven hundred tries. That is persistent. Some made five hundred attempts, some three hundred. Others had only fifty attempts. Then finally the shy ones: zero.

❱ ❱ ❱

Proof of concept, whether it is Kari Signor's spiked doughnuts or Patrick Darrow's RAG box, is difficult to demonstrate. With animal behavior and variability among animals, much can go wrong. But as hard as initial trials are, troubles are compounded when one brings new tools and techniques to the field. Nathan Lance's pen trials had proven that turbo-fladry was better than regular fladry, and that it was because wolves were smart and adaptable. They learned quickly. But how would one apply turbo-fladry in actual pastures instead of small pens?

To the ranchlands of Montana: Nate found study areas where wolf visitation was consistent or where livestock depredations had occurred in the past. He identified twelve forty-to-three-hundred-acre fields with forty to two hundred cows in each. As per usual scientific convention, control pastures were unprotected. Nothing to do there but monitor—walk around looking for tracks. The six treatment pastures were surrounded with miles of turbo-fladry. The strands of red flagging danced in the wind like millions of matador capes, but they were backed up with the punch of two thousand volts.

During the course of the study, there were no losses in turbo-fladry-encompassed pastures or in the designated control pastures.[21] Wolves did attack and kill on three nearby fields, however. One cow succumbed to wolf teeth in an adjacent field. In another unfortunate event, two particularly unlucky llamas were moved out of a protected pasture and to another one. One llama was killed while the other managed to escape with injuries.

Nate's study made one other important leap that is too often missing from biological studies. He wove people into the process—specifically, the local ranchers. Fladry did something to wolves. What was its effect on people?

For the final element, Nate surveyed the ranchers directly. The vast majority of ranchers, more than 80 percent of them, said that they would welcome more testing of such techniques on their property. In the heart of wolf-resistant Montana, barriers were being broken down. It took a willingness to communicate and a certain amount of charm, but if fears were assuaged, attitudes about wolves actually could change.

There were limits, of course, because ranchers are businessmen, too: 100 percent of the producers thought that electrified fladry was unaffordable and too expensive. For Nate as well, it was expensive, at $2,303 per kilometer for materials, and another thirty-two man-hours per kilometer to set up and maintain. If they had to pay for it, none of them would use it, the ranchers said. If there was cost sharing, or more specifically, if the technique was provided free of charge and free of responsibility, opinion shifted from 0 percent supporting the method to 67 percent saying they'd be likely or very likely to use it. Still a long way from 100 percent, but a vast improvement over zero. Cracks in the monolithic status quo of intolerance and war were appearing. Humans could learn too.

CHAPTER 8

CLOSE, BUT NOT TOO CLOSE

Altering Territories

There is a fence that stretches from one side of Australia to the other.[1] The Aussies constructed it to exclude dingoes from sheep range. Exclusionary systems don't always have to be so large and expensive, however. They can be simple bomas, corrals constructed from thorny branches to exclude African predators, or complicated chain-link fences with overhangs and underground aprons.[2] New World scientists began formalizing the study of fences for coyotes as early as 1909.[3]

In some ways, large predators are easier to fence out because there are usually fewer of them relative to small ones, and their size prevents them from slipping through minute holes that are difficult for humans to detect. However, larger animals do have greater strength and may require much more extensive constructions. Generally, if a resource to be protected is confined to a small area, a fence-type barrier can be constructed relatively easily.

Then do we need only to construct some fences? Around chicken coops, certainly. Some pastures as well. Electric fences are extremely successful for protecting commercial beehives from bears, and there are many occasions where some form of fence will be an excellent choice. In other scenarios, they are much less useful. There are aesthetic costs, for example, in making an idyllic farm pasture look like a fenced-off penitentiary. Would it be possible to build and maintain a fence around entire farms, ranches, and allotments? Perhaps. National Parks? I shudder at the thought.

Even if fenced and isolated reserves are big enough to hold our predators—tundra wolves and adult grizzly bears may use home ranges as large as a thousand square miles—they will be forced to live on what are essentially island patches. As conservation theory dictates, such island populations are more prone to extinction by the chance introduction of disease or by poor environmental conditions when compared to widely dispersed animals. If the truce we pen in the war with predators means essentially to jail them, can we expect their populations to survive into the foreseeable future?

Great fences and physical barriers certainly have a role, but there is danger in their symbolism, too. I worry that if we keep a few wild places with corridors between them, then it will seem more acceptable to pave over or plow every bit of land not dedicated purely as wildland.

I worry that we are not thinking about ways to incorporate ourselves into ecosystems and are favoring setting ourselves apart from nature instead.[4] Fences set us and nature further apart at a time when we need to be reconciling with nature's creatures.[5] Fencing parks perpetuates the notion that all we need are enough big areas where predators can live and nature can go on, but that is like jam in a jar. Nature preserves, similar to the real fruit, are not the same thing. If we continue to set the natural world apart from the overall populace, it will lose its value, no matter how loudly conservation biologists lament.[6]

Establishing reserves is not working anyway. Where predators are most at risk is where they interface with people, especially at the perimeter of parks and preserves.[7] For rare, large predators, reserves will probably never be big enough, and movement beyond their edges will continue to lead to the deaths of individuals and sometimes the decline of species. Mordecai Ogada and colleagues note in their paper in *Conservation Biology*, "Reducing the numbers of predators shot, speared, poisoned and trapped by people is the single most pressing need to halt global carnivore declines."[8] Resolving conflict can best be achieved not by trying to completely separate, but rather changing how we react to interactions.

If we want to have predators in perpetuity, we need to have more of them in more places, not fewer in smaller spaces. Shattering the myth that humans and predators must be kept apart is one of the greatest challenges to conservation biology. But how can we live closer together while setting our common stage in such a way that we can avoid stepping on each other? How do we live close, but not too close? The answer, in part, is by understanding better how the animals themselves divide up the landscape.

The sine qua non of coyoteness or wolfness is the function of the family group: the pack. The social bonds within the pack are reinforced by tail wags, bared teeth, and festivals of howls. The pack is a brigade whose purpose is to dispense with intruders and defend the territory's food resources. It is much like the human system of countries and armies.

If territorial behavior depends on food, what happens if we attack the root of a predator's motivation by toying with food resources? What if, rather than trying to repel predators from important resources, we used food to attract them—to lure predatory species *away* from livestock? Would it work? Or would if fail when fat and lazy coyotes or wolves failed to protect the edges of their lands from intruders bent on eating livestock?[9]

Julie Young examined these questions during her PhD studies. She too was a picture of rugged femininity and representative of the new diversity that will eventually change fundamental approaches in wildlife biology. "I don't like guns," she said off-the-cuff to me when we were riding together one day, "but my dad had us shoot and I'm a really good shot . . . but my dad also said that if a gun is out, something is going to die. So I don't like them."

Pragmatic, with black pony tails pulled tight on either side of her head, Julie trapped, collared, and mapped out the territories and social structure of coyotes at the Welder Wildlife Refuge in southern Texas. For an alternative food supply, the local butchers provided her with discarded cuts and bones from meat markets in Sinton.

Her first hypothesis: satiated from the four hundred pounds of meat she provided for them each week, coyotes would decrease their predation rate and abandon large parts of their home ranges.

Fat and lazy, they'd prefer to allocate their time near the predict-able supplies of steaks and chops. Home ranges would shrink and trespassing would increase.[10]

In short, coyotes don't read the textbooks: the territorial bound-aries held, their sizes remained stable. There were some differ-ences at a smaller scale, because coyotes with the supplemental food shrunk the sizes of their core areas, but they didn't change how they defended the overall territory. They ate well and spent time at the provisioning sites, but they kept their day jobs. Trespassing did not increase. The carcass dumps did not send the social structure and distribution of predators on the landscape into disarray.

Stepping back and approaching from another angle, Julie col-laborated with her predecessor, Bill Andelt, who had studied coy-otes on the Welder Wildlife Refuge in Texas two decades before.[11] Julie and Bill shared extraordinarily unique datasets that docu-mented coyote movements at the same site, but with a quarter of a century between them. Comparing notes, they made a surpris-ing discovery: Julie's coyotes' home ranges looked like the Olympic Rings laid on the map, one next to the other with minimal overlap and little interstitial space. Andelt's map from the 1970s stacked over Julie's nearly perfectly. More than five generations of coyotes separated the datasets, yet the division of the land between coyote kingdoms had stayed nearly the same. Territories were predictably stable through time.

If we can predict something in time and space, we can avoid it. Grazing patterns of livestock can be adjusted around the historical activities of predators.

◢ ◢ ◢

If territories provide stability and predictability to a landscape, what happens if an animal is removed? Does removal of an individ-ual wolf or coyote create ripples of destabilizing effects throughout the population?[12] What happens to the other animals on the sur-rounding landscape?

For fourteen years, scientist Mike Jaeger concentrated on the who's who of predation and coyote removal at a single site: the University of California's Hopland Research and Extension Cen-ter.[13] In the 1990s, Jaeger watched for sheep kills and then used intensive radio telemetry to identify which coyotes were the culprits. The first clear trend to emerge was that most sheep losses (89 percent of lambs) were caused by adult breeding pairs of coyotes. Not every coyote was a sheep killer; in fact, relatively few coyotes feasted on lamb. The majority of coyotes primarily killed rabbits and rodents, actually benefiting sheep by removing some of their herbivorous competition. It was typically a few older and bolder coyotes that were responsible for sheep kills, particularly those with large families and more mouths to feed.

The researchers also came to understand that coyotes that killed sheep were also better at avoiding human control methods. Coyote control preferentially removed the "good" coyotes, but left the repeat offenders, and the most destructive coyotes had become the most difficult to kill. As shown in the research Jaeger guided, the number of coyotes that were removed had no correlation with lamb loss;[14] predation continued regardless of widespread removal *until the actual culprit was taken.*[15] In the numbers game of the war on wildlife, coyotes were winning because the lowly and harmless infantry were being picked off by human defenses, while the learned and immune special ops platoons feasted on lamb.

Lethal removal had a small window of effectiveness, lasting only forty-three days before a new coyote claimed the vacant spot.[16] Jaeger argued that management could be more efficient and perhaps effective for even longer than forty-three days if we targeted the behaviors and removed only the guilty animals, instead of trying to kill any coyote we could put a bead on.

Lynne Gilbert-Norton continued her own finely focused investigations into sociality and territoriality as well. She teamed with Ryan Wilson, the PhD student who succeeded Julie Young at the Welder Wildlife Refuge. Working closely, Ryan and Lynne developed a sibling-like relationship of competition and support. They ribbed each other constantly with a shared brand of dry wit.

Red-headed and fair-skinned, Ryan had a complexion much better suited for the glare of a computer screen than that of the Texas sun. He was a particularly intelligent and productive scientist, learning complicated statistical analyses, writing, and navigating the peer-review process with aplomb. Ryan's success with publishing provoked simultaneous pride and envy in Lynne, who was an expert at coordinating people, conversations, and social events, but had more difficulty getting her ideas and experiments through the wringer of the scientific journal peer-review process. (She teased him, creating lovingly hilarious pet names that I ought not repeat here.)

Although they focused on problems from different angles, their complementary work better revealed the whole picture. Together, they built another study to examine a commonly promoted method for repelling territorial predators: artificial territories.

In the popular Disney movie of the book *Never Cry Wolf,* Farley Mowat famously peed a ring of his own urine around his campsite to ward off a nearby pack of wolves.[17] Lynne and Ryan wanted to test the notion: could creating an artificial barrier for wolves and coyotes, and perhaps cougars or bears, be as easy as urinating?

Scent-marking behavior is ubiquitous in mammals. For most species—humans being a notable and tragic exception—the sense of smell is a primary means of communication. Glandular and other body odors become signposts for olfactory-aware animals. Simple marks, such as urine and scat, provide a costless means of defending a territory and likely prevent dangerous confrontations with would-be intruders.

Can we create "bio-boundaries" that keep territorial predators away from livestock? How would coyotes respond if we tried to fake a new territorial boundary?

Lynne and Ryan performed two experiments to examine the hypothesis that coyotes would avoid an area delineated by human-placed coyote scent-marks.[18] Putting GPS collars on his coyotes in Texas, Ryan indirectly observed the free-ranging animals as they visited areas he delineated with coyote urine. He found pastures that were suitable for holding sheep and set about using an eye-dropper to place scent marks at regular intervals around them. For controls, he walked around similar plots, but left no coyote-relevant marks. The collars recorded the coyote's locations every few minutes, creating a bread-crumb trail on the map. Lynne, for her part, directly observed the responses of her coyotes at the Predator Research Facility to similar lines of coyote urine. She made Patrick do the dirty work.

Analyzing the data, Ryan determined that coyotes visited the artificial territories three times as much as control plots. They also spent more time wandering through the experimental areas than through the unscented control boundaries. His drops of coyote urine evidently said something like, "Nya, nya—we're on your turf!" which probably pissed off the locals.

Ryan's dots on the map brought real-world rigor, but indirect evidence. He had no ability to watch his subjects and record their behaviors. That part was Lynne's job. When her coyotes detected the scent, they shot toward it, heads down. They appeared to be gathering every bit of information they could about the intruder. Coyotes were attracted indeed, actively pacing across and through the boundaries of the simulated territory. Like Ryan's free-roaming coyotes, Lynne's coyotes visited artificial territories nearly twice as many times as when the technician walked the control boundary without perfuming it with coyote urine.

The experiment wasn't a failure in its inability to prove that artificial scent marks would repel coyotes. In contrast, Lynne and Ryan were onto something. There was a difference between control and treatment plots. The coyotes paid attention to the artificial scent marks. Their behavior and movements were altered. Scent marks were relevant; both of their studies showed that. For predator management, however, the important lesson was that if we were to use scent marks for our benefit, they would have to be used to attract, rather than repel, territorial predators.

The actual signals that coyotes used to repel each other and keep territorial boundaries constant through time is a more complex combination of invisible cues. A real bio-boundary could require howling and scratching, and perhaps dandruff from an intruder's pelage, or other chemical signals still unknown to humans.

Back in the 1980s, James Till and Fred Knowlton were just beginning to understand how indirect effects of sociality and territoriality could influence predation behavior. They noticed that when dens were found and coyote pups were killed, predation on domestic lambs ceased.[19] They hypothesized that sterilized coyotes would kill few if any lambs. They went on to predict that territoriality would exclude interlopers that would attack sheep.

Their results led to further research on both wolves and coyotes. With wolves in Alaska and Canada, initial studies indicated that the animals maintained territoriality and other behaviors after being sterilized.[20] They even appeared to live longer.[21] But could sterilization be used more broadly to prevent pups and therefore reduce predation on sheep?

A helicopter crew flew over the Deseret Ranch of northernmost Utah, net-gunning coyotes. "Muggers," as they are called, jumped from the open doors and tackled the entangled critters, then hobbled and muzzled them for handling. At the direction of Cass Bromley, the graduate student working on the project, the captured coyotes were shuttled out of state to the waiting staff at the Bear River Veterinary Clinic in Evanston, Wyoming. There, the ability to reproduce was taken from some of them.

For the study, coyotes were plucked from their territories and assigned as treatment or control animals. Treatment coyotes were surgically sterilized, while the controls went through "sham" surgeries: they underwent the same surgical procedure, except that their tubes were touched and not tied. Sham surgeries were done to control for any possible influence of flying or, for example, infection or change in appetite due to surgical procedures. After being allowed the night to recover, each coyote was returned to its original home territory.[22]

After sheep were grazed through both control and treatment packs, the losses were summed. One sheep was killed in the treatment territories. In the controls, however, eleven sheep were killed. Sterile packs killed 0.38 lambs per week, but intact packs killed an average of 2.95 lambs per week. Even with such an effect, the approach could be readily criticized because it took so much effort, involving helicopters and expensive biologists. How many years would it have to be effective to pay off?

Bromley calculated the answer. The cost to sterilize each coyote, including helicopter time, surgeries, technicians, and supplies, was $560/animal. Multiplying out, the cost of sterilizing a coyote pack was $1,680. Using the difference between the two treatments as the amount of loss averted (1.96 lambs killed/week) and stretching it over a summer grazing season (sixteen weeks), Bromley figured that about thirty-two lambs would be saved by treating an allotment in this way. Multiplying by market values: $1,792 of lamb-loss was prevented. The cost to surgically sterilize the coyotes was a little less than the amount saved. The process was economically feasible in the first year, but because coyotes are long-lived, similar savings could be expected to continue for several years.

Sheep operations are small and operate close to margins. Saving $2,000 a year is not a complicated concept but, with this approach, coyotes become part of the solution. It is a paradigm shift that will be difficult for many to process: protecting sheep by letting coyotes live.

Getting such complicated messages across was a struggle, too. Cass's advisor, Eric Gese, had tried to explain the research to one of the local ranchers. Gese described the experiment—how they captured coyotes, sterilized them, and returned them to their territories. He explained how the treatment animals would not have any pups, and how the sham-surgery coyotes would have their typical five or six. With fewer mouths to feed, the coyotes would need less food, which meant they'd be less tempted by domestic lambs.

The work seemed overly complicated to the rural bystander, who would have thought it odd to have a coyote in hand and not kill it. The rancher responded, shaking his head, "Sterilizing? You got it all wrong. They're not screwing the sheep. They're killing the sheep!"

Encouraging the use of nonlethal methods isn't only about biology. It is also about psychology—if not more so. The method that Bromley was trying—reproductive control—required a complicated explanation. It demanded several steps of reasoning and logic that didn't fit into a sound bite as easily as *a dead coyote can't kill a sheep.*

While biologists spend their time considering problems on the level of populations, regions, and evolutionary change—concepts invisible in everyday existence—ranchers deal in the absolutes of the here-and-now. There was enough precipitation or not enough. The forage was good or poor. Coyotes killed or did not. The lamb was alive or dead. To be successful, wildlife managers have to come more than halfway into the livestock owners' world. The reasoning must be obvious and results clear if novel methods are to be embraced and not simply ridiculed.

Coyotes and wolves are known for their territoriality, as are adult tom cougars. Bears, however, move from place to place as different foods become available during the spring, summer, and fall: from carrion, grasses, and forbs to fruits, berries, and nuts as the seasons progress. So we approach bears differently.

For me, surveying Wisconsin cornfields was like stumbling through crop circles left by an inebriated flying saucer pilot. There would be one massive tangle of broken stalks, then paths of destruction emanating into the field at random points around it. Kicking through stubble and flattened corn, Dave Ruid, the local Wildlife Services district supervisor from nearby Rhinelander, was showing me some of the impacts of black bears. He and his supervisors wanted to know if the Wildlife Services program there was effective, and I was invited to examine the issue.

When we first pulled to the roadside, I had scanned the edge of the farmer's cornfield and was unimpressed. We walked past an empty culvert trap—empty because the bear it trapped the night before had already been released into the Chequamegon National Forest earlier that morning. Ducking into the field, we followed an ursine path into the monoculture. A little chunk was taken out of the edge of the plot, where a few rows—perhaps two meters across—lay on the ground, trampled. Some plants still had the ears on them. Others had ears missing, and still other ears were half eaten and discarded next to the stalk from which they were ripped. The magnitude of the onslaught was invisible from the nearby farm road, but within the field the devastation was dramatic. You had to be close to the damage to feel the impact.

"There are a ton of bears around here," I remarked, stating the obvious. Dave smirked.

A fed bear is a dead bear is the refrain, foretelling a bear's ultimate end after it becomes accustomed to anthropogenic food sources. Habituated bears are destructive and potentially dangerous. Bears are particularly challenging because they range widely, adapt quickly to changes in food resources, and alter their behaviors to avoid or adjust to humans. They'll travel far and wide to access concentrations of food. They shift and alter too, adapting when there are obstacles: to eat our food, while avoiding being chased by humans, bears will switch from the "wild" diurnal pattern to a crepuscular and nocturnal activity pattern. They also pass on survival knowledge between generations, as mothers teach their cubs the locations and timing of certain crops.[23]

In the Midwest, bears have adapted to use such new food sources as short-maturity corn crops. Damage can be particularly significant. In one study, 55 percent of surveyed farmers reported crop losses from bears, with an average annual bear-related loss of 11 percent of corn and oats.[24] To a farmer in Wisconsin or Minnesota, the economic impact of bears could be compared to that of a flood, or to a seasonal swarm of locusts.

In response, the State of Wisconsin instituted a program that provides damage prevention assistance and partial compensation for crop losses from wildlife. In the program, the US Department of Agriculture's Wildlife Services wears a white hat—distancing itself from the death campaigns on coyotes in the West (even Wildlife Services is more complex and multifaceted than the purely evil entity it is often painted to be).[25] Wildlife Services employees work cooperatively with the Wisconsin Department of Natural Resources and County Land Conservation Committees to provide bear damage abatement. The program is not one of pure protectionism, it is also of pragmatism. Participants are required to allow the application of nonlethal damage abatement methods, especially translocation. In return, they are provided compensation for their agricultural losses. The responsibility for damage is thus shared among all participants. During 2006 and 2007, 161 farms were enrolled in the program and damage was assessed at $216,092.[26]

The practice of translocation is controversial among modern

wildlife managers who argue that it simply moves a problem from one field to another. It just causes more conflict elsewhere, or does nothing because bears quickly return to the site of capture. Our task was to assess the Wisconsin program. We were charged with determining what proportion of translocated animals were recaptured right back where they started.

A culvert trap is little more than a large tube on a trailer. The trigger is released when a bear tugs on bait in the rear of the trap and gravity slams the guillotine door shut. Once closed, the trap is hooked to the back of a government pickup and towed away. In the Wisconsin program, the trap is taken into public land to the north. Away from the farms, the specialist hops onto the top of the culvert, out of reach of the bear, and pulls up to open the door. Bears typically leap out in a full run, having endured the rather frightening experience of capture, enclosure, and highway travel.

We wanted to know which bears were which and if they returned. The major hurdle was not only the time and expense it would take to collar or tag the five hundred bears that were moved each year in Wisconsin but also the prohibition on drugging and handling bears for fear of human health concerns (there was some worry that a bear could later be harvested and eaten, with remnants of dangerous drugs in its system). To overcome this hurdle, we found a different way to identify animals, using newly developed genetic methods. For each bear captured, specialists acquired a tissue sample using special biopsy darts and a CO_2 pistol.

The sharp end of the biopsy dart is a tiny, hollow tube that, when popped into the hindquarters of a bear, incises a small tissue sample before it falls free. The shot is considered as painless as a flu shot, and a sample can be safely taken without anesthetizing the bear. The tip is unscrewed and the sample stored in a vial of ethanol for shipping and analysis.

After a few seasons of endless hours in the lab and field, we found our effort proved the obvious: there were lots of bears. From the samples, Karen Mock, a geneticist at Utah State University, identified 520 individual animals that had been captured in the fields. Each had been moved 25–37 miles from the site where they were causing damage, but the proportion of bears that came back was low. Only 4 percent of translocated bears returned. Such a low recidivism rate meant that translocation worked.[27]

Why did it work? Why didn't the bears come back? They weren't moved very far, especially in bear terms. The answer had to do with timing.

Corn is most attractive to bears during the milk stage—when kernels are mostly yellow and contain milky white fluid; at that time they are soft, tender, and delicious morsels. The stage occurs a few weeks before the plant matures and forms hard kernels of field corn. As it turns out, moving bears just a few miles resets the order of food courses. The bears *could* move back, but by then the corn isn't attractive, so they don't. They switch over to the next round of forest food types.

The power of translocation for any carnivore is less about the physical distance, and more about the timing of the action. If the period of conflict is short enough, translocation will prevent depredations.

Using wolves as an example, the pressure to eat domestic calves is highest in the few weeks before elk calves are on the landscape. Relief comes when spring brings more wild food in the form of elk calves—taking pressure off of the domestic sources. Cougars that follow deer down into towns in winter only have to be dissuaded for a few weeks, too. Temporary solutions can provide long-term effectiveness when a fundamental aspect of the conflict is temporary—which is often the case in conflicts with mammalian predators. Know your opponent. Choose the time and place of your battles.

CHAPTER 9

ANIMAL HUSBANDRY

Sometimes It's About Money,
Sometimes It's Not

Few human activities are as ancient as raising sheep. The vocation is of extreme biblical importance, especially in the Christian tradition: the pastor (from the Latin meaning *shepherd*) and his congregated flock. Abel, Abraham, Lot, Isaac, Jacob, Rachel, Laban, Moses, and David were all shepherds. Mary gave birth in a manger to the Lamb of God.

In the dusty town of Las Cruces, New Mexico, a band of modern-day woolgrowers invited me to present ideas about new methods for preventing coyotes from eating their sheep. We discussed the pros and cons of various methods, but they were most excited to hear what the future might hold. There were so many potential new repellents and even toxicants.[1] Everything was on the table, and it was inspirational to see young shepherds facing forward, wanting to continue their way of life and resist what looked like an inevitable slow death by feed-lot beef and petroleum-based fibers.

Sheep and their wool were integral to survival as the North American continent was colonized by Europeans. Tallies in 1867 placed the number of sheep in the United States between 40 million and 50 million head. Numbers rose and fell through the years. The United States achieved a peak of 56 million in the wool-hungry war year of 1942. Immediately after World War II, the number of sheep dropped to about half—30 million head—through the 1950s, and then fell into precipitous decline, with recent counts down to about 6 million sheep—10 percent of historic highs.[2]

Reasons for the decline of the industry in the United States are complicated and include the growth of synthetic fibers as well as globalization and an influx of cheap lamb—nearly half of US consumption comes from imports, mostly Australia (about 68–70 percent) and New Zealand (about 30–32 percent).[3] To protect livestock in places such as southern Australia, toxicants including Compound 1080 are unabashedly flung throughout the environment at a rate of 70,000 baits per year.[4] This practice has been illegal in the United States since the 1970s, so our citizens export the guilt of environmental impact to other countries while voraciously importing the benefits of their use.

Predation is undoubtedly a factor, but was it the cause of the US sheep industry's decline? No, concluded Kim Berger, a biologist at the Wildlife Conservation Society's Teton Field Office. Examining sixty years of data for correlations, Berger's economic analysis found that whether or not sheep were raised in areas with coyotes (eastern versus western states) had little bearing on the number of sheep raised. The negative impacts that were shrinking the industry, she concluded, were production costs (wage rates and hay prices) and market conditions (lamb price). Given the economic writing on the wall, sheep producers tended to identify predation loss as the last straw, a final reason to quit the business and, sadly, to sever their touch with the land.

Are today's sheep producers anachronistic biblical throwbacks who should be allowed to fade? Or do they have a unique and valuable connection with the land and livestock that dates from the beginning of civilization? If we lose that connection to the land and animals, are we losing some primary element of humanity? Interacting with the Las Cruces shepherds, I felt the honesty and purity in their passion. Their way of life was not touted as a spiritual quest, but I could see that it was. Their bond with the land meant so much more than economics.

Stately, plump, the sheep industry representative addressed the shepherds. His suit was of a western cut, but contrasted against the worn jeans of real rural-wear it struck me as the urban foppery of a poseur. He outlined the national organization's achievements. At the top of his list was his political protection of Wildlife Services' multimillion-dollar federal funding. He continued to explain, in a self-congratulatory tone, how his efforts to provide subsidies to sheep producers would not only continue but would increase. The shepherds smiled politely and thanked him with a sense of southwestern hospitality.

The only question I remember being asked of him came from a middle-aged woman with the fortitude and strength to want to raise her family in the sheep business.

She spoke plaintively. Honestly. "We don't want people just giving us money or doing this all for us," she said. "All we want is to be able to help ourselves."

The representative answered with a blank stare.

Conflicts between predators and livestock would end if we just got rid of the livestock, wouldn't they? According to the Center for Biological Diversity, the US government could save $128 million per year by not administering grazing lands as it does.[5]

But is it that simple? Humans need protein. We like lamb, but we eat a lot more beef. If not eating beef means plowing over grasslands, damming more rivers, and irrigating vast rows of soybean monoculture, I am convinced such a "cure" is worse than the disease. Cows are a tool that can be used wisely to turn nonirrigated and wild forage into protein. Humans can't convert grass and sage into usable nutrients in the way that ungulates can. Managed carefully, livestock can produce our protein in an environmentally harmonious way. Granted, completely decoupling meat production from the land by irrigating crops and trucking the plethora to cattle feedlots in Florida is the worst combination of all and not what I am advocating.[6] Nor am I assuming that there are no environmental costs to cattle production. What we are investigating is how to pragmatically balance human and biological systems so that we optimize human quality of life (which includes both the availability of inexpensive food and the continued existence of complex ecosystems) while minimizing environmental conflict and loss of predators.

The problem is not as hopeless as it sometimes seems. Our livestock industry can change. By some measures, the ecological impact of beef production has actually lessened. The carbon footprint per billion kilograms of beef in 2007 was 16.3 percent less than it was for beef production in 1977.[7] There has been a 12 percent reduction in water use and a 33 percent reduction in the amount of land required to produce beef. These may be good things, but the trade-off is an expansion of factory farming, which makes animals into machines for the sake of ruthless efficiency: further evidence of the disconnect between ourselves and the natural systems that we ultimately need to produce our food.

There is room for further improvement in the industry, but minimizing ecological impact is seldom cost-effective unless there are direct economic incentives. So, then, whose problem is it? Is the environmental cost of livestock solely the burden of the livestock owners? Is it only a sheep problem? A cattle problem? How do we actually address the worries and concerns of those who feed us?

"Isn't there anything else I can do to protect my calves?"

Ed Cummings was worried. Although the recently invented RAGs were set, he knew they couldn't be placed everywhere or work forever. He was worried about the long term. Ranchers seem to be always worried.

Ed had a situation that was fairly typical for ranchers in Montana. They had pastures for calving, where they could watch their herds and help with difficult births. The difficulty arose when the land greened in the spring and the calves were large, and ranchers grazed the animals onto adjacent public land allotments.

I suggested that just because high-tech methods and electronics were available to help, they were not the only options. Some methods were more complicated—or at least less intuitive—than others, so it took a little thinking. Some approaches hadn't been used or tested enough to be recommended, but still deserved consideration. Everything has costs, and there is no single, simple solution. There are, however, a variety of options that livestock producers can investigate to minimize loss while living with predators on the landscape.[8]

There were strategies at the periphery that work at least for coyotes but could perhaps be adapted for wolves, bears, or cougars. There was animal armor, for instance.

Different predators had different preferred methods of applying the coup de grace. Bears leap, chase, and swat, breaking bones in the back and neck before clamping down their jaws. Cougars stalk and attack from cover, launching onto the backs of their prey. They bite the head and the base of the skull, often puncturing it, commonly breaking the neck. Coyotes work from the underside, attacking livestock around the throat. They grab and crush, compressing the trachea until their prey suffocates.

An innovative method for protecting livestock is the use of a plastic collar that prevents canids from being able to grasp and choke sheep—the King Collar. This novel approach to animal armor was developed in South Africa to protect sheep from jackals. The manufacturer claims that the light and thin, but slippery, collar prevents a jackal from gripping the cheek and biting the trachea. Another device, the Vichos anti-predator collar, incorporates a chemical repellent in its construction. When punctured, the device dispenses a formulation of 3 percent capsaicin oleoresin. The hope is that the hot sauce in the collar will condition predators to not attack sheep, but in controlled conditions coyotes figured it out; they altered their method of attack, hamstringing and killing from the other end.[9]

Many more options for protecting sheep and goats from coyotes exist, but they require some bending of traditional values and approaches. Livestock owners have long contended, even to violent extremes, that they are either "sheepmen" or "cattlemen."[10] However, mixing the sheep and cattle into a "flerd" can have several benefits. Cattle are bigger, scarier, and more aggressive, at least to small predators such as coyotes. Such mixing has been shown to reduce coyote predation, and it may also improve efficiency of forage conversion into animal protein.[11]

Sometimes there are other factors that attract predators too close to livestock. Regular carcass removal and sanitation around operations may help to lessen the density of nearby predators and thus the severity of predation, especially in grizzly country. Coyotes and wolves are attracted to meat piles, too, but after arising from hibernation, hyperphagic bears are attracted from miles away. If carcasses are too close to living livestock, a few kills may be too hard to resist.

There are other huge attractants for scavenging predators, too. Highways are a smorgasbord. In Montana, the department of transportation cleans them of carcasses, and then turns the carnage into usable compost.[12] Seth Wilson, with the broad-missioned conservation group Blackfoot Challenge, documented how the group extended carcass pick-up and composting to ranchers—mainly to keep grizzlies from being drawn down into valley grazing land.[13] The total number of carcasses removed since 2003 was 4,300. They opened a second carcass composting site in 2010. Factoring in contributions and donations toward the program, the cost per carcass is $22. Thus it is not that expensive to turn a predator-attracting problem into a flower-feeding solution.

Another option that some cattlemen have is to alter the timing of breeding for their cows. Predators are often more likely to kill livestock when there are pups in the spring. If livestock are bred earlier in the season, calves and lambs are larger earlier and less vulnerable to predation when coyotes, wolves, and bears are on the prowl. The breeding cycle for domestic sheep can't be altered as much as that of cattle, and ultimately seasonality in market prices is a factor, but the economics of seasonal predation can be optimized too.

Finally, in talking with Ed Cummings about various options, we touched on another possibility—night penning—that he found particularly interesting. Dairy cows are amusing in their daily routines, happily jogging to their home barn when it is time to be fed and milked. It is a migration less majestic than the swallows' return to Capistrano, but every bit as magical. Beef cows could do the same with a little extra effort, if they were fed in the evening closer to the homestead. During the day, they could trot themselves to more distant and vulnerable pastures where they were more susceptible to predators. At night under lights, near barns and homes, they'd be protected. The practice is common with herded sheep, but has been thought to be too labor intensive for spread-out cattle. Indeed, for cattle on the range it is difficult to imagine, but for cattle in a pasture awaiting green-up, it isn't too much of a stretch in terms of labor.

A method of both first and last resort is compensation. If cattle owners are just running a business, would payments end their dyspepsia in the face of losses to wolves?

It is not that simple.

The Defenders of Wildlife created the first private compensation fund for wolf losses in North America, and the fund made its first compensation payment in 1987. The hope was that by taking away economic impacts, the fund would end legitimate opposition to wolf recovery by western ranchers. By 2003, the Defenders program had paid over $270,000 to more than 225 ranchers who had suffered wolf kills. Ed Bangs, the recovery coordinator at the time, said, "This program should be a model for others who want positive solutions for complex environmental issues. The livestock compensation program has made wolf recovery more tolerable to livestock producers and has made wolf recovery more easily attainable."[14]

Helpful at the time certainly, but compensation has not become the ultimate solution since the business of raising livestock isn't just about money. Perhaps it should not be a surprise that small business owners are often more proud of what they do or create than how much money they make, and such payments can be a mixed blessing—or worse.

Compensation is certainly a good thing because it acknowledges the hardship that people who live closer to predators experience. It can provide a psychological buoy, but ironically, it can also be a psychological anchor. Programs tend to pay for confirmed kills only, and confirmation requires a series of steps from the rancher in finding the kill, protecting the evidence, calling in a wildlife professional to determine the cause of death, and filling out forms until finally, perhaps, a check arrives. Each step in the process is a cost in dollars and headaches that impinge upon the effectiveness of compensation programs.

Pride is a part of the mixture, too. I have heard ranchers say, "I don't raise calves to feed wolves. I am in this business to feed people." The sentiment is deep and real, a sense of nobleness and purposeful importance among agriculturalists that is all but lost in modern-day urban culture.

Ranchers will say that throwing money at a problem is not necessarily a solution, especially because farming and ranching are not purely economic propositions. They are passions. Many farms would be worth more as housing tracts—surely to the detriment of the predators that we are concerned about—than they are as farms. To some, the idea of compensation is nothing short of a bribe, an insult.

The Wisconsin Department of Natural Resources, using funds acquired through check boxes on tax returns and from sales of a wolf license plate, created a compensation fund for damage from predators. Between 1976 and 2002 there were 121 incidents. The department offered compensation for livestock, farm deer, pet dogs, and hunting hounds. Between 1984 and 2002, $263,085 was paid to claimants. Reflecting rural pride, one livestock operation that was offered $22,700 refused to accept it. More importantly, did compensation change attitudes or opinions about predators? The short answer is no: those who had been compensated for their losses to wolves were not more tolerant of wolves than were their counterparts who alleged a loss but received no compensation.[15]

❧ ❧ ❧

If there are so many nonlethal methods for livestock owners to use and so many people who are willing to donate millions of dollars to the cause, why are guns still overwhelmingly the go-to method?[16] What if there was a market incentive that pressured producers to live with, rather than wage war on, predators? Is it even possible, given the age of fast-food and cheap, short-lived consumables, to care about not only where our food comes from, but how it affects predators on the landscape?

Value meals are born out of feed-lot efficiency, with little room for grass-fed yearlings that grow slowly on the range. Hyperefficient food production has no tolerance for predatory species that eat calves before they can be trucked away for fattening.

Is there a way to sustain the inexpensive production of affordable food? A way in which extra efforts are made to use nonlethal methods in dealing with predators, in which people work with, rather than fight against, landscapes and wild animals? A way that involves changing attitudes?

❧ ❧ ❧

"Even Walmart is incorporating more eco-friendly options," asserts Abigail Breuer of the nonprofit organization Wildlife Friendly.[17] Abigail is hopeful, but pragmatic. It startles me to hear the words *Walmart* and *eco-friendly* in the same sentence. Again, one has to learn to let go of preconceived notions.

"Building economies to save ecologies," Abigail says. "The idea of coexisting with wildlife and being predator-friendly is not really that new. A concept called 'Predator Friendly' actually started before its time, back in 1991. It got little bits of press and interest, but it was so futuristic that it lacked support and infrastructure."

One problem with such efforts relates to history and culture. There were small-town expectations about acceptable behavior around animals. As Patrick Darrow had described previously, killing a coyote was a social norm: one goes to church on Sunday and one shoots at a coyote in a field. "If you did Predator Friendly," Abigail observes, "you would be a pariah to the locals sometimes."

For generations, it was automatic to rail against cougars, coyotes, bears, and wolves. It would take a special person to say publicly that there could be better ways to do things than how his or her grandfather did them. "Predator Friendly was more like a support group than a market-based model," Abigail says.

The Predator Friendly label, and the fundamental core of the concept, meant a livestock producer completely swore off lethal methods of predator control. It meant especially living with coyotes, as opposed to killing them as a rule. Displaying the label meant a producer had changed how livestock were managed. It was the antithesis of how the West was won and fortunes were made. Such thinking was heresy. "There were threats made to the families of those that practiced predator-friendly ideas," Abigail says.

The Predator Friendly label persisted, at a low back-burner simmer, among those who swore to raise their livestock without killing predators. The loose organization and its label languished on uncertain footing for years. In 2004 it was adopted by the Predator Conservation Alliance, an outspoken advocacy group that transformed into Keystone Conservation in 2008. The idealized notion of peaceful coexistence remained alive, but the supporting resources and the management ability were limited.

Several other hurdles lay ahead of predator-friendly boutique livestock operations. The link to the marketplace was weak conceptually but also physically. Small producers, who typically resided in the Rockies, were far from the eco-product-hungry markets of urban centers; the locals were against them and the potential supporters did not know they existed. The approach simply could not get off the ground.

Abigail contrasts the start of Predator Friendly with the creation of infrastructure for the Certified Organic label. "Organic" took years and a wealth of funding to get off the ground, but only "handfuls of thousands" had been injected into Predator Friendly.

That part of Abigail's narrative coalesced. "The producers that were thinking about more wildlife-friendly operations needed a marketing umbrella. They needed a label that would attract business expertise and funding," she says. They needed objective endorsement of third-party certification, too. They received it when

Predator Friendly merged with Certified Wildlife Friendly in 2009. A mechanism for much-needed support and discipline had become available. "The standards have been revamped and producers are being linked to markets all over the country and even the world," she concluded.

Abigail touts Elephant Pepper as the current best model for success. In Africa, farmers are economically secure only if they can coexist with elephants. Wildlife Friendly developed a cash crop, in the form of products using chilies, which its affiliated farmers grow around other crops to create a nonlethal barrier that elephants are reluctant to browse through. The ripe chilies are made into Elephant Pepper. The completion of the economic circle occurs when Elephant Pepper is stocked in the aisles of progressive stores, such as Whole Foods. Can scientists and students find Wolf Pepper . . . Cougar Pepper . . . Bear Pepper . . . Coyote Pepper— nonlethal solutions at least initially financed by foodies?

Texts such as Michael Pollan's *The Omnivore's Dilemma*, along with magazines, radio shows like National Public Radio's *The Splendid Table*, and even the term "foodie" itself prove that ideas about the quality of food, its sustainability, and the morality of its production have become part of the zeitgeist. We have become more interested in how our food is produced, but Wildlife Friendly must make economic sense, too. Fortunately, as Abigail notes, "The health and sustainability lifestyle market sector is growing. It's also a market composed of a class of people that pay disproportionately more for products."

The movement is not likely to be as big as the organic label, so it may be best to temper expectations. Wildlife Friendly labels won't substantially increase the margins for a pound of beef. If a product is not inherently above others in quality, it won't appeal to quality-minded consumers. Most Wildlife Friendly producers are already organically certified and selling top-end products. The Wildlife Friendly label makes the product one better, standing out a little more on the shelf to attract the consumer. "The label provides access," Abigail asserts, and offers a long-term approach to building a market more than maximizing immediate returns.

The nascent Predator Friendly concept has spread to boutique farms and ranches across the country. Thirteen Mile Lamb and

Wool in Belgrade, Montana, is one of the earliest subscribers, boldly and bravely coexisting in the heartland of "the only good coyote is a dead coyote" mindset. The label is growing from coast to coast, from the Living Earth Farm in Eugene, Oregon, to the Ayrshire Farm in Upperville, Virginia.[18]

When Predator Friendly began, livestock producers had to swear off any lethal methods and promise strict adherence to an idea. Since the label has become part of Wildlife Friendly, it is more conceptual and flexible. A livestock producer must still acknowledge and embrace certain ecological habits, including valuing wildlife species. Producers need to agree to try to live and let live as much as possible. They employ guard llamas, donkeys, and dogs. They reduce vulnerability to predation in the way they schedule pasture rotation and in how they time calving during cycles when predation pressure is lower. Wildlife Friendly requires more than marketing to cities. It takes rural marketing, too. It means a necessary change of mindset in North American agricultural towns. If enough people take the approach, everyone can't be a pariah. Nonlethal methods, instead of all-out war, can become the new first approach, the new normal.

CHAPTER 10

THE POWER OF EMOTION AND
THE NEED FOR KNOWLEDGE

Nonlethal approaches to predator management require a fairly intricate understanding of animal behavior. Luckily, there are dedicated scientists who are rising to the challenge, but complex realities mean that success will not be effortless. Each situation and animal is different, and we must be prepared for unforeseen issues and difficulties.

For example, Lynne's experiments were simple in design: to obtain the extra morsels of food, coyotes only had to step on the correct pedal a sufficient number of times. The coyotes figured out the game, but they all did it their own way, adding elements that complicated her analyses. By coincidence, Missy had bumped against the pen's fence the moment before food dropped. Fooled into believing that the fence also held power in reward, she added the fence-bump behavior to the foot-stomping repertoire. Her rhythm became step-bump, step-bump. Chewy created a repeated series of movements elaborate enough to resemble a line dance. Given uncertainty, coyotes, like other animals, become frustrated, then receive pleasure when they obtain their rewards. In a mechanism they share with people, coyotes create biases and preconceived notions through emotional responses. They even form elaborate superstitions.

The inherent emotional conflict of protecting creatures that would think nothing of killing and eating one of our own, of loving ani-

mals that can be so dreadfully dangerous and brutal, leads to vocif-
erous discussions among graduate students. Everyone's approach
to the problem is as individual as they are. Lynne was vocal and
opinionated, partial to hard cider. Patrick Darrow, following the
Word of Wisdom in Mormon Doctrine, swore off strong drink,
but not strong thoughts and opinions. He and Lynne were oppo-
sites, but both of their perspectives were crucial.

Members of the rural working class, such as Patrick, would have
reason to resent the urban conservationists: Folks in the cities demanded to be fed and enriched by farmers and ranchers spread
over the countryside. The agriculturalists carry the emotional
and financial burden of the damage that predators cause. Distant
urbanites reap the benefit of someone else doing their hunting
and gathering for them. They export the cost of large predators,
maintaining the grizzly bears' extirpation in California, while
through legal means insist that more roam into Patrick's backyard
in Idaho.

For Patrick, being raised at the interface of people and wilderness was tough, but to my mind, being raised away from the natural world—and never hearing the howl of a wolf or even a coyote
yelp—is tragic. Life is too short to not experience a shiver over a
cougar track in the snow, its paw placed on the print you left an
hour before.

I worry about our cities. They are great comforts for humanity, but people wall themselves away, a highway and a driveway at
a time, from the world that created them. To sum up my conversations with Patrick, it had become clear to him that God did not
simply create the earth for humans to destroy. Deep and pivotal
in Mormon Doctrine is the idea of free agency. That is, God does
not control human will—it is entirely up to every human to make
the right choices, or not. Carrying out this reasoning leads to the
conclusion that God will not fix our mistakes on the earth for us.
He'll present us with the challenge. We may have strong emotional
responses one way or the other, but by learning and applying our
knowledge we will be able to choose the right path. It's just that it
remains our responsibility to do the work.

Patrick, Kari, Lynne, Nate, Arion, and the others had demonstrated biological effects and observed successes and failures. Their work reflected a broad diversity of approaches, achievements, growth, and learning. Integral to the predator paradox is the wide variety of people it touches. Solutions do not rest solely on the shoulders of the livestock producers who interact directly with coyotes, bears, wolves, and cougars. Farmers and ranchers are crucial indeed, and we have discussed ways to empower them. We have tried to develop a number of real and potential management options to protect livestock, ways to de-escalate the battles. But the solution depends on all of us. We all have a certain responsibility to understand and act on wildlife issues, rural and urban, distant and near.

What the body of evidence shows is that the war will not end with an immediate, unconditional surrender. It will be a long process and will not result in a painless heaven for both predators and people. Any book or organization that promotes an end to the problems of predator and people management is selling a fairy tale. We can end the war on wildlife, but there will always be a need for diplomacy and for enforcing the compromises. We will have to make difficult choices. We will have to move from our own self-righteous comfort zones and truly consider the perspectives of others who live in a very different world.

❦ ❦ ❦

What is more adventurous and romantic than a rugged individual in the remote Himalayas tracking the mythical and precious snow leopard?[1] The narrative is straightforward: the gorgeous cat is a perfect, tragic victim, a princess imperiled in a high, snowy kingdom. As with wolves, unseen in the distant West, the villain tormenting them is abstract, distant. Resting a world away in tamed surroundings, we can't really feel the painful twinge of responsibility. All we have to do is write a check to the heroes and we become saints. Such beasts and quests, however, are the outliers in the relationship between humans and animals. As dire and unfortunate as such distant situations are, they aren't the crux of the matter. Indeed, compassion and desire to save mythic, far-away beasts is a much easier task than the one directly before us.

I retain a frustrating memory from my graduate days at the

University of California, Berkeley. It tends to piss people off, because I can't relate it without sounding sanctimonious myself: A driver steps out from one of the wonderful Berkeley restaurants. He seems comfortable and pampered, and his sandals show that he's got nothing much besides leisure to worry about. He moves toward his polished car, and the sticker on the back bumper implores, "FREE TIBET." There is a disheveled one-legged man begging on the sidewalk. The sandaled man doesn't notice the indigence at his feet and, giggling from the buzz of artisan beer, walks past. Maybe it's just me who gets so annoyed. It seems inherent in human nature to send a check to a distant organization and display its bumper sticker as a badge of honor, rather than to make real concessions on our own sidewalk. Think globally, ignore locally.

The annual incomes of many city-based conservation groups are in the tens of millions, often with major portions of their budgets dedicated to fund-raising, and focusing on crises rather than solutions. Conservation groups are absolutely essential and do very important work, and I do not want to focus too much criticism on them, but the annual spending for the multiple state and federal agencies that actually manage the wolves among us—$3,345,618 for 2012—is far less than that sent to a myriad of advocacy groups.[2] Engaging in cultural displacement behavior, we assuage our guilt by spending more on symbols and on the bludgeon of lawsuits than on the biology. As a biologist, and not a lawyer—yes, it bothers me. It is indeed important to support national conservation organizations for the work they do, but even more important to actually act locally and individually: to consider ecological costs of various types of food and to interact directly and frequently with policy makers.

The predator paradox is about the interface of humans, animals, and environment, and not about an easy, clear morality from a distance. It is about the people and animals that we impact, either directly or within a few degrees of separation. When a wolf, bear, or coyote eats a calf—or when we kill a predator in retaliation—it sends ripples through our psychological and economic zeitgeist. There is no sugarcoating. It ought to be uncomfortable, but the distance of having others do our killing for us has warped our perceptions.

One of the most uncomfortable things that wildlife managers must do is lead or attend public meetings about predator management. The affairs, especially when mammalian predators are on the docket, tend to become vituperative eruptions, with both sides disrespectfully targeting the predator biologist in the middle. What the managers need is a dominance of rational thought, not the screaming histrionics of radical fringes on either side. Real solutions can happen only if those with passion for predators, as well as passion for reason, become part of the process, both in a larger, political way as well as in an everyday way. Advocates also must know enough about predators and how to interact with them to be able to make effective arguments and points. Luckily, there are energetic educators among us.

🠓 🠓 🠓

"This isn't just cutesy-pants stuff we do in visitor centers," Mary Ann Bonnell, lead naturalist for the City of Aurora, Colorado, says. "There are 35,000 people in the area, and 98 percent don't think they'll need wildlife education, but they are going to get it."[3] Even over the phone, Mary Ann exudes enthusiasm and energy, and the excitement is contagious. "I'm at heart an educator, with a degree in biology."

She described the day that sent her down her current path. On April 30, 1998, Mary Ann was a ranger at Roxborough State Park, near Englewood, Colorado. The three-mile climb up Carpenter's Peak was a popular hiking trail, and it was there that she encountered Andy Peterson, not long after he'd been attacked by a cougar. First on scene, Mary Ann tended to the thrashed and bleeding man. She aided with his rapid evacuation for medical help. He had fought back and survived, but needed seventy staples to patch his wounds.

"He was jogging with a white t-shirt around his waist," she recounts, painting the image of a tan young jogger as a verisimilitude of a white-tailed deer. "We had displays and signs about cougars and nature at the park, but the information was about stuff like how big mountain lions are." The displays were about interesting natural history, and not about potential interaction. "There wasn't anything about safety," Mary Ann recalled.

Conflicts with such predators occur with the randomness of a game of chance, with great lags of nonevents punctuated by cataclysms of pain and fear. For the majority of us, living in urban areas and suburbs, interactions with wolves are more or less impossible. Bears and cougars are invading, and their attacks are front-page news, but it is the coyote that haunts Mary Ann—and suburbanites from coast to coast.

Mary Ann's opinion on coyotes is best described as pragmatic acceptance. We are not getting rid of coyotes, so we have to prevent them from breaking bad. Coyotes in cities and suburbs are normally like shadows, their presence only indirectly inferred by the disappearance of house cats, but some small percentage pose a greater threat. "We only hear about coyotes when they are behaving badly, but not every coyote behaves badly, and we have to get that message out too," Mary Ann asserts.

Aurora's goal is one of proactive education, but the challenge is to engage people and provide them with information before they help to create a problem. In what she terms a "full court press," Mary Ann and her group proselytize to school groups and at parks and public events. She tours incessantly the wilds of the greater Denver metropolitan area to find anyone who will listen to her presentation.

There is hope edged with a sense of exasperation in her voice when she describes her work: "My second month for the city was trying to calm down a grieving pet owner who was yelling and crying over her dead dog. For many urbanites these days, pets equal kids." In the area surrounding Aurora, about twelve attacks or losses of pets to coyotes or lions are reported each year, but Mary Ann thinks the actual number is higher. The more frustrating aspect is how predictable the scenarios are: "It was a little dog. The owner's house was right next to open space where coyotes were known to be. It was 11 p.m. when they let it out by itself." Many of the attacks and losses could be avoided easily, if people just knew how to act around wildlife.

Mary Ann's favorite audiences are Rotary Clubs. It gives her an opportunity to be outgoing and entertaining, but it also allows her to reach out to people who would otherwise not know that they were part of the problem—or the solution. "The Sierra Club folks are already engaged," she observes. The people who strike out to hike and camp already have some interest in educating themselves about the natural world. At the expanding interface between wilderness and manicure, though, people are more surprised to see wildlife than they ought to be. They ought to know what to do when encountering a coyote or cougar there. She encourages them to be "SMART."

"*Stop*," the city's instructional materials begin. "*Make* yourself look big; stand tall and raise and wave your hands. *Announce* yourself; launch into a string of vulgar expletives or gibberish—whatever comes to mind. *Repeat*, and finally, *Teach* a neighbor to do the same. The City of Aurora wants everyone to remember to be SMART with coyotes in town. If everyone does this, coyotes will retain their fear—and avoidance—of humans."[4]

Mary Ann discourages other actions, such as throwing things at coyotes. "Most people don't have anything, especially anything appropriate, to throw," she says. People start scanning the ground and looking for a rock or a stick. This breaks eye contact with the coyote. Then they kneel or bend over, which is exactly the wrong message to send to the predator. "I think that's exactly when the lion got close and attacked Andy Peterson," she says. "Besides, most people can't hit the animal. Whatever they throw becomes an item of interest and the coyote goes to sniff it, actually *attracting* it. Worse, I know someone who threw a sandwich."

In a moment of panic, people often don't think things through. They need training themselves, to know that they are responsible for that coyote's behavior. "If someone is a big-league pitcher and has a baseball or rock in hand already, then they should throw it," Mary Ann advises. If not, the message should be to simply wave their hands and yell, keeping eye contact.

A sufferer of what she describes as "tragic optimism," Mary Ann acknowledges that the need for sound public education will not go away. Indeed, it's an uphill battle. News outlets too often follow the "if it bleeds, it leads" model, delving into—or even creating—controversy, rather than helping to educate people on what they can do to prevent the problem. Mary Ann laments the messages people are bombarded with in other media, too. Nature shows depict people interacting with wildlife in improbable ways. They pet, caress, and befriend—the exact opposite of what must occur in cities, suburbs, and towns if people are to be safe.

Mary Ann admits being frustrated not only with the press, but also with advocacy groups that seem more willing to criticize than help. "I send them our plan. They don't comment. When the plan goes public, they pounce, creating controversy for contributions," she said.

It's disingenuous, and sometimes it can be difficult to tell who is out to help and who's just out for profit. With people and predators encroaching on each other, now more than ever we need to disseminate accurate and useful information. People should be SMART. They ought to know what to do when they encounter coyotes, cougars, wolves, or bears.

In our gallery of predators, the American black bear follows the coyote as the next most significant danger to normal folks. These bears are far less dangerous than their larger cousin, the grizzly, but there are far more of them, ranging from coast to coast, campground to campground. Stephen Herrero and his colleagues analyzed interactions between humans and bears from 1900 until 2009 and found that at least sixty-three people were killed by black bears during that time.[5] Over three-quarters of the deaths occurred in Canada and Alaska, but most—86 percent—occurred after 1960. Why the increase? It wasn't that some places had high bear populations, corresponding to lots of attacks; statistically, it was the opposite. Interactions between bears and people increase when people enter the woods, using campgrounds and summer homes.

Black bears are generally peaceful, more likely to climb a tree than charge if they suddenly find themselves in close quarters with humans. Yet as we have seen, they are individuals, too. Upon encountering a human, some bears will be calm and confident, others will panic and run. On rare occasions, black bears will be aggressive, even predatory.

Black bears are most likely to cause problems in campgrounds where people have left out food or otherwise enticed the bears to return. The damage is mostly to property, as bears tear into coolers or cars. Such campground or roadside bears will usually flee when people bang on pots, yell, and otherwise make the site an unpleasant and noisy place to be. Everyone in the camp should join in, although campers should keep children and pets close, of course. Campers should lunge and appear threatening to a campground bear, but not approach closer than five yards.[6]

Never run if you encounter a bear on a trail. With all predators, running may provoke an instinctual behavior to chase, resulting in a pounce and a kill. Be large, flare out your jacket, and retreat slowly and confidently. If you are on a narrow trail, move perpendicularly off the trail so the bear can pass. Always position yourself such that both you and the bear can retreat. Escape routes ease tension for both of you.

A male black bear may weigh 300 pounds, and the animals are no strangers to killing and eating meat. A difference between black bears and species such as coyotes is their pattern of attacks. Aggressive coyotes have usually been habituated through feeding. With black bears, however, some individuals simply consider humans as potential prey. In 90 percent of deaths that Stephen Herrero and his colleagues analyzed, predation was the motivator for the bear.[7]

There is safety in numbers; 91 percent of bear attacks were on parties of fewer than three people. A little more than a third of attacks were influenced by human garbage and only 8 percent of the attacks were by females. The notion that mother black bears are the most dangerous isn't strictly true—it is actually hungry males. Male bears acted purely as predators in 88 percent of the attacks that Herrero investigated. If a black bear attacks you, the probable motivation is predation. You must fight back. Do not play dead. Fight back with every ounce of strength. Punch its nose, eyes, and throat. Kick and do whatever you can to slow the attack. There is a trend among hikers to bring collapsible walking sticks. This is good. Such devices can make good weapons.

How does one tell if a black bear is stalking, with an eye on a meal, or if it is wary and worried? Black bears that are being defensive don't growl or raise their hackles, they commonly huff or make a popping sound with their jaws. They may stand on their hind legs, huff, and stick out their tongue to sample the air. In that situation, an attack is probably not imminent and it is best to stay calm, make noise ("Hello bear, hello bear, I'm going to go home now . . ."), and back away slowly.

Black bears that are being predatory, unfortunately, don't announce themselves. They stalk, and are silent and quick. Thus, people should not be overly afraid of predators, but they ought to be vigilant in black bear country, which is almost everywhere. The level of vigilance should be similar to the awareness you have when withdrawing money from an ATM. It's not likely that you'll be mugged, but you are more vulnerable if you are not paying attention to your surroundings and let someone sneak up behind you.

When hiking with dogs or children, keep them close and under a watchful eye. If there are several adults, put them at the beginning and end of the hiking party, with the children in the middle but never out of sight. It is not necessary to ring bells and blast air horns constantly. Normal trail badinage and panting will alert black bears before you come upon them.

When camping, have an adult in the tent and not a lone child. Predatory black bears have been known to bite through a tent and pull out a sleeping child. Food should be prohibited from tents. Its odor will tempt bears to swipe into the fabric. Sleep with a light and a knife nearby. The chances of an attack are extremely remote, but chance does favor the prepared.

Grizzly bears and black bears are similar in many ways, but strikingly different in others. Grizzlies are typically less timid and more curious. They are bigger and more aggressive and more likely to kill a person in an encounter. They are much rarer, especially in the contiguous United States, and thus are much less likely to be encountered by the general populace than are black bears.

When hiking in grizzly country, it is best to hike in a group, with safety in numbers, and to keep children in the middle of the line.[8] Be wary. Stop and look at vantage points. When moving through areas where vegetation is thick and the line of sight limited, make noise. Make it a habit to clap and holler when approaching blind corners.

Bear bells? Some people attach bells to their packs, so they make some amount of noise with every step. Experts aren't certain whether bears clearly hear the high-frequency and relatively gentle sound of the bells above the rustle of leaves, the babbling of brooks, or the whoosh of water. Is the ting of a bell salient to grizzlies? They probably are not detrimental, but they are not a repellent or a replacement for being aware of one's surroundings.

❧ ❧ ❧

Dr. Tom Smith at Brigham Young University analyzed 269 incidents of human-bear conflicts in Alaska.[9] The data involved black bears as well, but most incidents involved the more aggressive grizzly bears. He and his colleagues found little evidence that the use of firearms influenced an interaction's outcome—be it no injury, an injury, or a fatality. There is likely some emotional solace when one carries a weapon, but the feeling can be misleading. The most important aspect for predicting a safe outcome, Smith concluded, was how people used their brains, not their guns.

Bear spray tends to be the preferred active defense for people exploring bear country. The Interagency Grizzly Bear Committee published a position and informational paper on the use of bear spray to deter grizzly attacks.[10] Experts agree that it is as important to know how to use the spray as it is to have it. If used correctly, it will minimize injury in the event of an attack. The experts caution that bear spray is not 100 percent effective, nor is it a substitute for common sense, awareness, and proper camp sanitation in bear country. The point is to not get into a situation where you have to use it. If necessary, however, properly used bear spray can fend off a charging bear.

There are many personal defense sprays on the market, but the preferred product is labeled "Bear Spray" and lists the Environmental Protection Agency registration number on the front label. Bear Spray resulted from a tested formulation and delivery system designed for deterring bears. One uses it by aiming it at a threatening bear, beginning when the animal is about twenty feet away. The object is to use short, six-second bursts in a circular pattern to create a fog between person and bear.

❧ ❧ ❧

Tragically, more than half of people who are killed by cougars are less than four feet tall.[11] Cougars are known to focus on weak, sick, or vulnerable deer, and will select for human children when their goal is a meal. The cats tend to be crepuscular—active at dawn and dusk—but most attacks occur when people are out and about during daylight hours.

Victims are typically lone joggers and mountain bikers. The recurring theme of safety in numbers applies regarding cougar encounters, too. With children, the rule of keeping them between bookends of adults is particularly important. Keep small children within sight, and preferably within reach.

When I was a team member with Larimer County Search and Rescue, training as a handler with Search and Rescue Dogs of Colorado, I was called out on a multiple-day search for a young boy. On the evening of October 2, 1999, we headed up the Big South Fork hiking trail near Fort Collins, Colorado. A three-year-old had become separated from about a dozen church-group hikers.[12] He was said to have been running back and forth between groups of hikers who had become strung out along the trail.

Our team was told to search uphill as far as we thought it reasonable that a three-year-old would go, which kept us close to the trail, avoiding cliffs and areas of difficult passage that a three-year-old could not traverse. The highest any team went was about one hundred feet above the path. The search became more complicated after a National Guard Helicopter crashed on the site and operations shifted to rescuing the helicopter crew, but we kept looking for the little boy. We found no evidence, no clues. It was as if he had just disappeared. We worried that he had been kidnapped. The team's organized and active search for Jaryd Ataderyo was called off on Friday, October 8.

Years later, on June 4, 2003, two hikers were scrambling up the mountainside, far off-trail. They found sneakers and clothing. They knew the story of the missing boy and deduced what they had found. They were about 500 vertical feet above, and almost a quarter mile away from, where Jaryd was last seen. The clothes were identified as being Jaryd's by his father.

The boy was most likely dragged up into the rocks by a cougar and consumed.

Who knows how many times people have been watched by a cougar while walking trails? The lesson is that a resting cougar may not be able to help itself if a child runs down a path in front of it. The response would be instinctual and lightning fast. The lone child would seem to just disappear.

Cougar attacks are still incredibly rare, but they do seem to be on the rise.[13] They are almost exclusively predatory in nature. In fifty documented attacks on children from 1891 until 1997, only two cougars were motivated by rabies.[14] What should one do when encountering a cougar? The response depends in part on the level of the threat and whether a person is diminutive in stature or not. Seeing a cougar bound away across a trail or road is rare and magical. Very few people are lucky enough to have such an encounter. Alternatively, if a cougar does not immediately retreat but rather watches or stalks, follow the same rules as you would with the other predators: Stay calm. Never run. Face the animal. Pick up children or hold them close to you. Your calmness and touch may help to keep children from panicking or running. If a child is between you and the cougar, have the child stand still, and move toward the child. If the cougar stares intently, make yourself look bigger and retreat to a safe location. If the cougar still does not retreat, but appears to be staring intently and crouching or slowly stalking, throw rocks and sticks. Hold on to your walking stick—you may need it as a weapon. Yell, shout, and show your teeth.

If the cat is close, back legs twitching, ears focused forward—looking like a house cat about to pounce—an attack is imminent. Pull out a knife, a tree branch, binoculars, or a rock and charge at it, stopping out of its reach, shaking your weapon in its face. Pelt it soundly with a rock or any weapon you can devise. If attacked, fight back with all of your effort. Hit it and stab it with any weapon available, gouging at its eyes. If a cougar retreats after trying to attack a child, stay with and continue to protect the child. Cougars will focus intently on their prey and may return even after being deterred once. Keep the child close and retreat to safety, gathering potential weapons as you go.

Wolf range is limited relative to that of cougars, but in many ways wolves are more visible on the landscape. Biologist Mark McNay interviewed witnesses and classified eighty wolf encounters from Alaska and Canada.[15] Healthy, nonrabid wolves acted aggressively in slightly less than half of the events, and predation was the clear intent in three of them. All of the predation events were on children. It was also clear that injuries could have been much worse if adults had not intervened when the children were set upon.

In wolf country, the rules for hiking are similar to those relating to encounters with any of the other of our mammalian predators, and should come to be common sense. Keep children close and between bookends of adults. It is extremely unlikely that a person would encounter a wolf before it has detected an approaching human and retreated, but if a wolf is bold or habituated, the same rules apply as with all of the other predators. Look big. Yell. Throw. Never run—retreat slowly, keeping eye contact. If attacked, punch, kick, and fight for your life.

As humans and predators comingle, it should be obvious that it is not only the nonhuman animals that require management. In addition, interactions won't occur only in national preserves or in the remote wilderness of Alaska. They will also be at our doorstep, so we must make adjustments on the homefront, too.

When designing public parks or the interface between wildlands and a housing area, will we continue to create based on an aesthetic of what nature should look like, or will we consider and incorporate the processes of nature? Landscape architecture is another discipline that wildlife biologists need to infiltrate.

Back in suburban Colorado, Mary Ann Bonnell lamented: "Landscape architects have to be more creative with their designs . . . they create a park, put a pond in it with nice sloping beaches and plant palatable turf. So the geese take up residence and people begin complaining about their poop." But that is just the beginning of a landscape designed for conflict. "The planners make these long storm water conveyance corridors which become fingers of wilderness into the city," she said. The designs draw animals into our midst, injecting the reach of open space directly into parks and yards. "After the geese arrive, the coyotes arrive," she noted. Goose poop is a nuisance, coyote teeth are a physical threat.

Mary Ann became animated with the topic. "I want one more document slipped in the paperwork when you buy a house near open space," she said. Her proposal is part tongue-in-cheek, but with a very serious edge. "You can't sanitize open space," she said. "If homeowners live there, they have to agree that they are not just buying the view." Bonnell wishes for a world where people understand that wild areas have costs and responsibilities associated with them. They would sign a document accepting the burden. They'd have to agree that native perennials aren't weeds. They would sign a promise that they will supervise their dog, and not leave pet food and garbage out to attract coyotes or bears.

Cougars generally follow their prey, deer, down into developments. Designing landscapes with wildlife in mind can help prevent herds of deer in lawns and gardens, but homeowners must be knowledgeable and vigilant participants. Predators need cover, and not just food. Vegetative cover near yards and playgrounds creates comfortable places for cougars and coyotes to reside. Everyone living on the edge of open space should install and maintain motion-detection lighting. The disruptive stimuli will keep most wary predators away.

Ranchers in Montana ought to keep attractants like carcasses from their fields, and suburbanites should eliminate artificial food sources, like palatable shrubs and plants that could attract deer and subsequently coyotes, bears, and cougars. Pets, too, are an attractant, and they and their food should be kept in at night. Food left in and around cabins in the woods cannot be tolerated. Before locking up after a holiday weekend, campers ought to patrol their cabins and grounds, thinking like a walking stomach and eliminating attractants. Seemingly innocuous things like bird feeders are bear attractants, and a single chance feeding can lead to weeks and weeks of returns.

On a larger scale, too, we focus and funnel animals precisely where they shouldn't be. A highway perpendicular to a deer migration route will not only kill deer but coyotes, bears, and motorists, too. Will we make it standard practice to incorporate wildlife bypasses as roads and housing areas are built or improved? Far more development will happen in every state, but designing with the animals in mind will keep corridors and interchanges from Alaska to Florida open.

If we apply concepts such as disruptive stimuli and aversive stimuli, and—most importantly—mollify our irrational fears, we can have more predators in more places, without all-out war. If we are to have broad corridors and healthy populations, the interface between humans and carnivores should be soft and measured, not a razor-edged border. We can blend into the wildlands, and the wildlands into us.

A grizzly bear or cougar cannot live next to school grounds, but there is plenty of space between the schoolyard and nature reserve for gradations of tolerance. Using zoning, lands can be assigned into shades of use from integration and coexistence to uncomfortable tolerance and outright exclusion of predators when it is necessary.

In Wisconsin, for example, the northwest is full of farms and has a high potential for conflicts. Such areas are not appropriate for wolves, so quotas are high, with 147 wolves targeted to be killed on the two hunting zones there in 2013.[16] Other areas in the northeast are closed to hunting, or have a much lower quota. Wolf management zones neither eradicate wolves nor afford them extreme protection. Zones protect us and protect them by incorporating a land use policy that is variable, flexible, and pragmatic.[17]

Beyond implementing physical zones, we humans will have to negotiate emotional zones as well. Our deep emotions are another reason why conflicts between people and predators are not going to be easy to resolve, and why resolutions will not be painless. The symbols that we make of mammalian predators can become barriers, as isolating as any metal fence. We'll need to sort objective reality from emotionally charged symbolism and conquer irrational or counterproductive actions if we are to de-escalate and close divides.

There is a dangerous aspect of wolves that ironically has nothing to do with the animals themselves, but with our perception of them. In many ways, wolves are the same as the other predators, in that they are complex carnivores that intermittently stumble into a conflict with us. Oh, but wolves are so different, too. They charge a room with hate, fear, or reverence far beyond that of any other animal that I have dealt with. They are the subject of many more books, articles, and essays. They require a little extra discussion here.

In what is probably his most famous quote, Aldo Leopold, the father of wildlife management, describes killing a wolf. The scene is familiar to most in the field and appears in Leopold's *Thinking Like a Mountain*. Trigger-happy and hoping that fewer wolves meant more game, Leopold poignantly described the last moments of a wolf that he shot. He sees the "fierce green fire dying in her eyes." He adopts a tone of remorse for failing to think bigger and wiser, like a mountain would.

For a sense of clarity and streamlining of argument, an important detail was omitted from the previous account of Val Asher and the Sheep Mountain Boys. It was the story of a fourth wolf, their mother.

Capturing wolves in a pen is like chasing a mob of dazzling butterflies, except that each is ten times as fast and weighs more than eighty pounds. Carrying large nets while trying to swoop and pin, we had spread out among the four Sheep Mountain wolves, hoping to hold each one long enough to inject it with a chemical cocktail that would induce slumber. There were twice as many people as wolves. One biologist had an air pistol and a handful of drug-loaded darts. The wolves were panicked and our efforts were disorganized.

I gazed upon the fourth wolf. Her ears were furry black. Gold-green eyes set into a mask of mottled gray, her muzzle grew darker and darker until it ended in the ink spot of her nose. Underneath the strong line of her jaw, the fur was counter-shaded in white. She looked old and tired. She would stop, stand, study, and then run again.

It was the moment when a wolf and I had the conversation of death, but with the disturbing twist that she was the prey. I peered into the fierce green fire in her eyes that Aldo Leopold described in his own epiphany—when he questioned his own relationship and preconceived notions about predators. In his case, the eyes compelled him to urge us all to recognize our impacts on the species and land. He grew to argue that we ought to pursue an ethical application of management instead making a blind rush toward domination. It was a drastic change of thought. All predators weren't all bad all of the time. There was something less absolute.

In this, Leopold established a beginning. In acknowledging that there were costs associated with benefits, Aldo Leopold was a visionary. In the examination of the wolf's fire, however, in the compassionate study of the strength of her gaze, he missed something. Leopold fell short.

During our capture attempt, every dart went wide and stabbed the grass behind a panicked wolf. They bounded about, bumping each other, and caromed off the fence. One wolf finally dashed close enough and a net was upon him. Weaving the needle between strands, a biologist injected ketamine into the wolf's leg. Eventually, the wolf's two brothers and mother were pinned and sedated, too. The pandemonium lasted too long. Wolves were overheating, and we knew it, but there was no easier way to sedate the wolves and make them malleable enough to allow us to put collars on them. We needed the time to drill into the collars and attach the black box of electronics that would hang at the sides of their throats— blunted metal probes pressing directly against their necks, a strong contact for the transmission of an electric jolt.

We were fitting the collar when the mother wolf took her first labored breaths.

Called over, the veterinarian left the young boys to sleep

soundly, their eyes glassy and tongues lolling. He turned to concentrate on the adult female. There was a hesitation in his actions and concern in his voice. The wolf's body had peaked in excitement and panic, then plummeted into anesthesia. She struggled against the extremes, her temperature spiking, but she was stabilized. We backed away to let her recover.

Soon enough, her young were up and running, sporting their new collars and observing their mother from the far side of the pen. She lay groggy, listless, her gaze vacant. For hours afterward, Val fanned the she-wolf and kept the animal cool while its body metabolized and broke down the drug.

Ketamine is normally very safe, with a wide margin for error in dosages. It is used in humans, too. Small amounts in lollipops offer an effective preoperative medication for children.[18] In adults, ketamine has recently been touted as an effective treatment for depression.[19] At higher doses, it has been popular with the club crowd as Special K or, even less savory, as the date rape drug. Related to infamous compounds such as PCP, ketamine in still higher doses can produce extreme and terrifying hallucinations that lead to violent self-mutilating behaviors.

We could not tell what the she-wolf could see or feel as she lifted her head intermittently. We could not detect the visions that were playing behind the steel of her eyes. Perhaps she was studying the visage of Death.

I looked again into the wolf's eyes. I could see, in their dying glaze, the fierce green fire, too. But the moment was not one of some greater understanding of the universe. In the eyes of the wolf there was no magic, no calm dignity. In the eyes of the wolf was recognition: she had no control of her limbs. She had strange and terrifying creatures hovering above her as the world swirled into ghostly shapes of shadows and grays. The wolf shared with me more than it shared with Leopold's mountain. The vision behind the eyes was a mammalian emotion—a fellow feeling—and not the stoic permanence and wisdom of ancient granite. In the pale green fire that I saw that day was the piercing intensity of fear.

The experiment was supposed to be good for wolves. It was supposed to grant leniency on a pack that otherwise was slated for death. It was about finding a path to coexistence, where wolves could live adjacent to fields of cows, but know that killing the domestic animals wasn't worth the risk or effort. In the real world, it seems, no good deed goes unpunished. The death of the matriarch brought on a maelstrom of emotion. Also disturbing was the fact that as scientists we were stepping out of the box, trying something intermediate and compromising in a world bent on absolutes, but we had failed.

We had found the training collars, which we adapted to fit on wolves, in pet stores. The cover of the box had a prominently displayed logo, a ring composed of four white palms encircling profiles of beloved pets. The text below the graphics read: "The Humane Society of the United States." Then in fine print: "½ of 1% of net wholesale price of this product goes to support the HSUS."

A nonlethal approach to wolf management. Endorsed by the Humane Society of the United States. What could go wrong?

SHOCKING TREATMENT OF MONTANA WOLVES: This experiment is just the latest machination in USDA "Wildlife Services" agency's war on wildlife, waged in the name of a handful of livestock interests."
—HSUS *Humanelines* webpage, August 2000

There was a war on wildlife, indeed, and our training collar experiment was a Hail Mary pass at a solution, but it certainly wasn't a machination in the war. It was a first step toward détente, but the ironic attack by a supporter of the technology for pets was unforeseen. It was a demonstration that there weren't only pure heroes and evil, uncompassionate villains in the dance between humans and wolves. We could lose our heads by yielding to unrestrained emotions.

The portrayal of our work stuck. Firmly lodged in the public eye, the experiment prompted a deluge of news reports, then frank and direct e-mails featuring flowery language and inconsistent grammar, mostly directed at Ed Bangs, the wolf recovery coordinator who had sanctioned the experiment. The response focused on emotion and finger-pointing rather than on regrouping and rationally searching for solutions.

> Another wolf dead in your carnival of forced evolution eh, Ed, you contemptible fraud? Couldn't learn how to process the "stress," heat and poison you shot her with, eh? Not fast enough study? How is the shock treatment going on the others you've got penned up for "training?" The wolves in the West need you like the Jews needed Himmler, Ed.

Perhaps it is too difficult to not take sides in the war. Indeed, people fall too readily into angry *for* or *against* camps, rather than learning from setbacks. We have to accept that something has to give, that we can't enjoy the benefits of predators without accepting the costs and difficulties of managing them.

In our experiment, we were intermediaries, actors, and the wolves were unknowing subjects. They were wolves, so they weren't innocent, but they were wolves, so they weren't guilty. It is the recurring theme of wildlife biology: managing animals is difficult, but managing people is hell. In our interactions with predators, we will have failures, even given our best intentions, and we will have to be as persistent and clever as the animals we are working with.

The Arctic Crawler's monstrous tires dwindle in apparent size behind the polar bear that leans, contrasting, against them. Tourists gasp and point their cameras, anxious to store the images that are burning onto their retinas. Ensconced in a vehicle that combines bus and monster truck, the people are safe from an animal that would gladly swat and tear the gawkers limb from limb. People drop everything and come from all over the world to experience this rush.[20] Polar bears are massive, powerful, and extraordinarily dangerous, and people go to Churchill, Manitoba, just to be close to them.

A little more than a thousand people live in the town. They go to work. They raise families. They find ways to work around the bears, which invade the land after the ice of the Hudson Bay retreats in July. At first, polar bears listlessly wander the landscape, resting and composing themselves after the long winter on the ice. After the short, lazy summer, the bears congregate and roam around Churchill. They pace expectantly, waiting for ice to form on the Hudson so that they can ride the floes and fill their bellies with seal meat. It is a yearly event, as predictable—and sometimes as scary—as Halloween.

Halloween, indeed, is done differently in Churchill, with armed men patrolling neighborhoods while trick-or-treaters roam. It looks like an occupying army overseeing ghouls, ninjas, and zombies—all manner of costumes except anything all white and mistakable for a polar bear.

Polar bears, like the grizzly or their black cousins, are primed to find and acquire food efficiently. They find dumps, sniff houses and cars, and view people as snacks, which puts the residents of Churchill into a precarious position. The difference in Churchill is that the residents are not at war. They have adapted.

The natural resources agency, Manitoba Conservation, instituted the Polar Bear Alert Program. It does just about everything we want to accomplish with this book. In Churchill, officials protect people while ensuring the conservation of polar bears.

The program is proactive in nature and features a beautiful combination of the methods required to prevent conflicts before they are created: minimizing attractants, implementing zoning, and conducting nonlethal hazing of bears. Another essential component is education and outreach. Manitoba Conservation Resource officers visit classrooms annually to explain the bears' habits and to outline safety measures to children.

The town and former dump (closed in 2005) are bear-free zones, where bear intrusion is not tolerated. Bears outside of the buffers may roam freely, and visitors are expected to take their own precautions—most are protected by the immense crawlers. A hotline is manned twenty-four hours a day. If bears are reported in the bear-free zone, a chain of events is initiated. The Polar Bear Alert Team launches into action, deploying an array of scaring devices. They try to harass the bear and persuade it to move away from the area. If it won't move, they set a culvert trap, much like those used for their smaller cousins. If needed, bears are darted and immobilized chemically.

Then, they are off to D20: jail. The Polar Bear Holding Facility is used to house the potentially threatening bears. It isn't a rewarding stay, as they are not fed during their incarceration, but it allows them to cool their heels in air-conditioned cells until they can be released when, once again, the ice forms. There is room for twenty-three bears, but most years more than that are captured. The extras are drugged and helicoptered far from town to await the cold.

Churchill, Manitoba, is not a mirror for all of North America, but it is a model. There are aspects that make Churchill's approach easier: polar bears' annual incursion is predictable. The bears are easy to find, and they aren't inflaming passions while stealing livestock in the night. They are, however, the biggest and most aggressive predator in North America, and they enter a town hungry. Ultimately, it is the citizens' attitude that is the key: these people have figured out how to live with polar bears in a way that minimizes harm to people and bears alike.

The well-honed program provides proof of concept. Given the immensity and aggressiveness of polar bears, the people of Churchill have solved the most difficult and challenging case. Black bears are much easier to live with, and wolves are easier still, even cougars. Diminutive coyotes already live within urban and suburban settlements.

If people in Manitoba can learn to live with their predators, so can we.

We can end the war.

ACKNOWLEDGMENTS

Thanks to my son, Fox, for being a good sport about my obsession with, and desire to expose him to, the natural world, science, and the arts. I thank him for the inspirational sign he pecked out as a first grader, which hangs above my desk and says, "Good typing dad!" I thank Laura Wood at Fine Print Literary Management for representing me and for her encouragement and belief in me and my topic. Alexis Rizzuto at Beacon is a most patient and wonderful editor who reminded me that the "inspiration and writing of a book is like the falling in love part of a relationship, and the revision process is more like a marriage—it takes more work!" I thank her and Will Myers for reining me in when I overindulged as a scientist freed to write nonscientifically.

Joel Berger's insights were inspirational, and I appreciate his support at such an important time. Ken and Chris Krugler of the Nevada City bus stop posse kept me motivated at the earliest, difficult stages, as did support from Robin and Mark Selden. Curt Lyons and Florence Gans threw a few life-lines, and I much appreciate Caroline Lavoie's support and friendship. Thanks to Donna Barry for the photo shoot and Paige Pagnucco and Utah State for helping with local marketing. I thank Douglas Townsend and Virginia Gans at Treasure Hill Highlands Farm in New York for inviting me to their property. The passion of family farmers is so inspiring.

I respect many colleagues from Wildlife Services and have appreciated working with them through the years: David Ruid, Scott Barras, Stewart Breck, Eric Gese, Larry Clark, Diane Arnold, Mike

Bodenchuk, Mike Linnell, Jeff Green, Bob Willging, Rick Williamson, and so many more. I hope that the light in which I've portrayed them or their agency is taken in the context of a challenge to improve, and not as a personal criticism of them, their motivations, or their lives and values. I know that they are just trying to help, too, and I acknowledge and appreciate their efforts. The USDA Wildlife Services' National Wildlife Research Center provided most of the funding during my career as a federal research biologist, and I hope they may not only continue to fund research, but to also find ways to actively apply it.

Lynne Gilbert-Norton and Patrick Darrow were extremely gracious to allow me to pick on them in particular, and to document their growth from neophytes to professionals.

The list of those who were so important as I developed my thoughts is long: Karen Mock, Adrian Treves, and Diane Boyde (I wonder if she even remembers her speech, much less knows the impact it had on me at the time). I undoubtedly learned more from my graduate students than I taught them: Lynne and Patrick, of course, but also Dan Heffernan, Nathan Lance, Arion Vandergon, Kari Signor, Alex Metter, Julie Young, Stacey Brummer, and Ryan Wilson. The hospitality and patience of Francisco García Domínguez, Victor García Matarranz, Jaime Muñoz-Igualda, Jose Lara Zabia, Luis Mariano González-García y la profesora, and Mariana Fernández Olalla while I was teaching myself Spanish so late in life was phenomenal.

Those from the wolf world were instrumental in forming my thoughts and career: Adrian Wydeven, Peggy Callahan, Caroline Sime, Mike Jimenez, Val Asher, and all at the Turner Endangered Species Fund. We all owe much more to Ed Bangs than he gets credit for. I appreciate the tireless efforts and passion of Carter Niemeyer. Also, I appreciate the efforts of Suzanne Stone and others at Defenders; we may approach the world from different angles, but I think we have some common goals. Defenders funded my prototypes for the Radio Activated Guard, and I hope the investment will pay off one day. Mary Ann Bonnell, with the City of Aurora, is the type of person who is essential for resolving the predator paradox, as is Abigail Breuer. There are far too many friends, colleagues, and students who have shared ideas with me—or shouted me down when I was being stupid—to mention, and I apologize in that I will miss so many in these short acknowledgments.

I could tritely thank the coyotes, cougars, bears, and wolves for being there, but I know enough about them to know that they don't give a damn about me, and that's okay. Still, I find immense pleasure in learning about them, and they've nevertheless earned my gratitude.

APPENDIX

Species Reported as Killed Intentionally
or Unintentionally in USDA, Wildlife
Services Annual Table, 2011

Anhinga, American alligator, nine-banded armadillo, red avadavat, American avocet, badger, largemouth bass, bats (individual species not reported), black bear, beaver, unidentifiable birds, yellow bittern, Brewer's blackbird, red-winged blackbird, yellow-headed blackbird, eastern bluebird, western bluebird, bobcat, bobolink, red-vented bulbul, lark bunting, snow bunting, spectacled caiman, caracara, northern cardinal, red crested cardinal, catfish, feral cat, chickens, eastern chipmunk, chukar, American coot, double-crested cormorant, pelagic cormorant, brown-headed cowbird, coyote, sandhill crane, American crow, fish crow, northwestern crow, long-billed curlew, axis deer, black tailed deer, mule deer, red deer, sika deer, white-tailed deer, feral dog, Eurasian dove, mourning dove, spotted dove, white-winged dove, zebra dove, short-billed dowitcher, American black duck, bufflehead, canvasback, common eider, feral duck, gadwall, Barrow's goldeneye, common goldeneye, harlequin duck, long-tailed duck, mallard, common merganser, hooded merganser, mottled duck, Muscovy duck, northern pintail, northern shoveler, redhead duck, ring-necked duck, ruddy duck, greater scaup, lesser scaup, blue-winged teal, cinnamon teal, Eurasian green-winged teal, green-winged teal, black-bellied whistling duck, American wigeon, wood duck, dunlin, bald eagle, great egret, cattle egret, snowy egret, elk, American kestrel, merlin, house finch, fish (other), northern flicker, scissor-tailed flycatcher, guinea fowl, arctic fox, gray fox, kit fox, red fox, swift fox, black francolin, Erckel's francolin, gray francolin, American bullfrog, Atlantic brant, black brant, cackling goose, Canada goose, emperor goose, feral goose, Ross's goose, lesser snow goose, greater white-fronted goose, feral goat, marbled godwit, pocket gopher (all), boat-tailed grackle, common grackle, great-tailed grackle, pied-billed grebe, red-necked grebe, greater black-backed gull, Bonaparte's gull, California gull, Franklin's gull, glaucous gull, glaucous-winged gull, Heermann's, herring gull, laughing gull, mew gull, ring-billed gull, western gull, jackrabbits, broad-winged hawks, Cooper's hawk, ferruginous hawk, northern harrier, harris hawk, red-shouldered hawk, red-tailed hawk, rough-legged hawk, sharp-shinned hawk, Swainson's hawk, great blue heron, green heron, little blue heron, black-crowned night-heron, yellow-crowned night-heron, tricolored heron, glossy ibis, white ibis, white-faced ibis, white ibis, black spiny-tailed iguana, green iguana, black tailed jackrabbit, long-tailed jaeger, blue jay, scrub jay, Steller's jay, dark-eyed junco, red junglefowl, killdeer, eastern kingbird, western kingbird, Mississippi kite, white-tailed kite, red-legged kittiwake, horned lark, mountain lion, lizards (other), monitor lizard, Lapland longspur, black-billed magpie, chestnut mannikin, nutmeg mannikin, marmot, purple martin, eastern meadowlark, western meadowlark, deer mouse, house mouse, mink, northern mocking bird, moles (all), Indian mongoose, moose, patas monkey, rhesus monkey, common moorhen, moose, muskrat, myna, nighthawk, nutria, Virginia opossum, osprey, river otter, barred owl, burrowing owl, common barn owl, great horned owl, short-eared owl, monk parakeet, rose-ringed parakeet, gray partridge, collared peccary, American white pelican, ring-necked pheasant, Say's phoebe, feral pigeon, northern pikeminnow, American pipits, black-bellied plover, golden American plover, semipalmated plover, porcupine, black-tailed prairie dog, Gunnison's prairie dog, white-tailed prairie dog, pronghorn, quail (all), Gambels quail, cottontail rabbit, desert cottontail rabbit, feral rabbit, swamp rabbit, raccoon, black rat, hutia rat, kangaroo rat, Norway rat, Polynesian rat, common raven, ringtail, American robin, sanderling, least sandpiper, pectoral sandpiper, rock sandpiper, semipalmated sandpiper, upland sandpiper, western sandpiper, feral sheep, shrews (all), loggerhead shrike, warbling silverbill, hog-nosed skunk, hooded skunk, spotted skunk, striped skunk, Eurasian skylark, brown treesnake, garter snake, gopher snake, other snakes, Southern Pacific rattlesnake, western diamondback rattlesnake, venomous snakes (other), Wilson's snipe, Eurasian tree sparrow, field sparrow, golden-crowned sparrow, grasshopper sparrow, house sparrow, java sparrow, Lincoln's sparrow, savannah sparrow, white-crowned sparrow, Douglas' squirrel, eastern gray squirrel, fox squirrel, California ground squirrel, other ground squirrel, Richardson's ground squirrel, round-tailed ground squirrel, red squirrel, rock squirrel, western gray squirrel, European starling, black-necked stilt, bank swallow, barn swallow, cliff swallow, northern rough-winged swallow, tree swallow, violet-green swallow, mute swan, tundra swan, swifts (all), feral swine, black tern, caspian tern, common tern, gull-billed tern, least tern, California towhee, turtles (other), common map turtle, common musk turtle, common snapping turtle, painted turtle, wild turkey, snapping turtle, other turtles, voles, black vulture, turkey vulture, common waxbill, long-tailed weasel, weasels (other), whimbrel, willet, gray wolf, American woodcock, downy woodpecker, Gila woodpecker, golden-fronted woodpecker, bushy tailed woodrat, dusky footed woodrat, eastern woodrat, greater yellowlegs, and lesser yellowlegs.

NOTES

CHAPTER 1

1. Jon T. Coleman, *Vicious: Wolves and Men in America* (New Haven, CT: Yale University Press, 2006).
2. Marc Bekoff and Eric M. Gese, "Coyote," in *Wild Mammals of North America: Biology, Management, and Conservation*, 2nd ed., ed. George A. Feldhamer et al. (Baltimore: Johns Hopkins University Press, 2003), 467–81.
3. Stephen DeStefano, *Coyote at the Kitchen Door: Living with Wildlife in Suburbia* (Cambridge, MA: Harvard University Press, 2010).
4. Bekoff and Gese, "Coyote."
5. J. Frank Dobie, *The Voice of the Coyote*, 2nd ed. (Lincoln, NE: Bison Books, 2006).
6. Ibid.
7. John Steinbeck, *The Pearl* (New York: Viking, 1947).
8. Agricultural Statistics Board, "Sheep and Goats Death Loss—2010" (National Agricultural Statistics Service, Agricultural Statistics Board, US Department of Agriculture, 2010); Agricultural Statistics Board, "Sheep and Goats Predator Loss—2000" (National Agricultural Statistics Service [NASS], Agricultural Statistics Board, US Department of Agriculture, 2000).
9. Miika Tapio et al., "Sheep Mitochondrial DNA Variation in European, Caucasian, and Central Asian Areas," *Molecular Biology and Evolution* 23, no. 9 (September 2006): 1776–83.
10. Wendy Keefover-Ring, *War on Wildlife: The US Department of Agriculture's "Wildlife Services"* (Santa Fe, NM: WildEarth Guardians, 2009).
11. USDA Wildlife Services, "Table G. Animals Taken by Component/Method Type and Fate by Wildlife Services—FY 2008," in *Wildlife Services' 2008 Annual Tables* (Washington, DC: USDA/APHIS/Wildlife Services, 2009).

12. USDA Wildlife Services, *Wildlife Services Program Safety Review Evaluation of Current Safety Program and Identification of Safety Improvements* (Washington, DC: USDA/APHIS/Wildlife Services, 2008), http://www .aphis.usda.gov/.

13. Richard M. Nixon, Executive Order 11643 Environmental Safeguards on Activities for Animal Damage Control on Federal Lands, US 37 FR 2875 (1972).

14. Coleman, *Vicious.*

15. Donald W. Hawthorne, "The History of Federal and Cooperative Animal Damage Control," *Sheep and Goat Research Journal* 19 (2004): 13–15.

16. A. Starker Leopold et al., "Predator and Rodent Control in the United States," *US Fish and Wildlife Publications*, Paper 254 (1964).

17. S. A. Cain et al., *Predator Control—1971: Report to the President's Council on Environmental Quality and the Department of the Interior* (Washington, DC: Advisory Committee on Predator Control, 1972).

18. USDA Wildlife Services, "Table G. Animals Taken by Component/ Method Type and Fate by Wildlife Services—FY 2011," in *Wildlife Services' 2011 Annual Tables* (Washington, DC: USDA/APHIS/Wildlife Services, 2011).

19. Ibid.

20. *2008 figures*: USDA Wildlife Services, "Wildlife Services' 2008 Annual Tables." *2009 figures*: USDA Wildlife Services, "Table G. Animals Taken by Component/Method Type and Fate by Wildlife Services—FY 2009," in *Wildlife Services' 2009 Annual Tables* (Washington, DC: USDA/ APHIS/Wildlife Services, 2009).

21. Guy E. Connolly, "The Effects of Control on Coyote Populations: Another Look," in *Symposium Proceedings—Coyotes in the Southwest: A Compendium of Our Knowledge* 36, ed. Dale Rollins et al. (San Angelo, TX: Texas Parks and Wildlife 1995), 23–29.

22. David Quammen, "Planet of Weeds," *Harpers Magazine*, October 1998.

23. Paul Mackun and Steven Wilson, *Population Distribution and Change 2000 to 2010* (Washington, DC: US Department of Commerce Economics and Statistics Administration, US Census Bureau, March 2011).

24. Eric M. Gese et al., "Influence of the Urban Matrix on Space Use of Coyotes in the Chicago Metropolitan Area," *Journal of Ethology* 30, no. 3 (August 3, 2012): 413–25.

25. Robert M. Timm et al., "Coyote Attacks: An Increasing Suburban Problem," *Transactions of the North American Wildlife and Natural Resources Conference* 69 (Washington, DC: The Wildlife Management Institute 2004): 630–39.

26. Ibid.

27. Ian Austen, "Mother of Canadian Singer Killed by Coyotes Asks That the Animals Be Spared," *New York Times*, November 2, 2009.

CHAPTER 2

1. John K. Oakleaf et al., "Effects of Wolves on Livestock Calf Survival and Movements in Central Idaho," *Journal of Wildlife Management* 67 (2003): 299–306.

2. Agricultural Statistics Board, *Sheep and Goats Death Loss—2010* (Washington, DC: National Agricultural Statistics Service, Agricultural Statistics Board, US Department of Agriculture, 2010).

3. Agricultural Statistics Board, *Cattle Death Loss* (Washington, DC: National Agricultural Statistics Service, Agricultural Statistics Board, US Department of Agriculture, May 12, 2011).

4. Bryan M. Kluever et al., "Vigilance in Cattle: The Influence of Predation, Social Interactions, and Environmental Factors," *Rangeland Ecology and Management* 61, no. 3 (2008): 321–28.

5. Agricultural Statistics Board, *Sheep and Goats Death Loss—2000* (Washington, DC: National Agricultural Statistics Service, Agricultural Statistics Board, US Department of Agriculture, 2000).

6. Agricultural Statistics Board, *Sheep and Goats Death Loss—2005* (Washington, DC: National Agricultural Statistics Service, Agricultural Statistics Board, US Department of Agriculture, May 6, 2005).

7. Agricultural Statistics Board, *Cattle Death Loss*.

8. Mark Collinge, "Relative Risks of Predation on Livestock," *Proceedings of the Vertebrate Pest Conference* 23 (Davis: University of California at Davis, 2008): 129–33.

9. Associated Press, "Court Upholds Dismissal of Charges," *Casper (WY) Star-Tribune Online*, April 8, 2006, http://trib.com/.

10. Jon T. Coleman, *Vicious: Wolves and Men in America* (New Haven, CT: Yale University Press, 2006).

11. Gordon Grice, *Deadly Kingdom: The Book of Dangerous Animals* (New York: Dial, 2010).

12. "ADF&G Report Confirms 2010 Wolf Attack Fatality," news release, Alaska Department of Fish and Game, accessed August 18, 2013, http://www.adfg.alaska.gov/index.cfm?adfg=pressreleases.pr12062011.

13. "'Stay Calm': Woman Walks Away after Canada Wolf Attack," NBC News.com, March 20, 2013, http://worldnews.nbcnews.com/.

14. "Bear Attacks on the Rise, Raising Safety Concerns," NBCNews.com, August 18, 2013, http://worldnews.nbcnews.com/.

15. Stephen Herrero, *Bear Attacks: Their Causes and Avoidance* (Guilford, CT: Lyons Press, 2002); Stephen Herrero et al., "Fatal Attacks by American Black Bear on People: 1900–2009," *Journal of Wildlife Management* 75, no. 3 (2011): 569–603.

16. Herrero, *Bear Attacks*.

17. "Court Sides with Family of Utah Boy Killed by Bear," *Standard-Examiner* (Ogden, UT), July 19, 2013, http://www.standard.net/.

18. Raul E. Lopez and Ronald L. Holle, "Changes in the Number of Lightning Deaths in the United States During the Twentieth Century," *Journal of Climate* 11, no. 8 (1998): 2070–77; Kathy Etling, *Cougar Attacks: Encounters of the Worst Kind*, 1st ed. (Guilford, CT: Lyons Press, 2004).

19. David Baron, *The Beast in the Garden: The True Story of a Predator's Deadly Return to Suburban America* (New York: W. W. Norton, 2005).

20. *Living with California Mountain Lions* (California Department of Fish and Game, 2005).

21. Agricultural Statistics Board, *Sheep and Goats Death Loss—2005*.

22. Dorothy M. Fescke et al., "Cougar Ecology and Natural History," in *Managing Cougars in North America* (Logan, UT: Berryman Institute Press, 2011), 15–40.

23. Baron, *The Beast in the Garden*.

24. Wendy J. Keefover-Ring, "Mountain Lions, Myths, and Media: A Critical Reevaluation of 'The Beast in the Garden,'" *Environmental Law* 35, no. 4 (2005): 1083.

25. Ibid.

26. Hank Fischer, *Wolf Wars: The Remarkable Inside Story of the Restoration of Wolves to Yellowstone* (Helena, MT: Falcon Press, 1995).

27. M. D. Jimenez and S. A. Becker, eds., *Northern Rocky Mountain Wolf Recovery Program 2012: Interagency Annual Report* (Helena, MT: USFWS, Ecological Services, 2013).

28. William J. Ripple and Robert L. Beschta, "Wolves and the Ecology of Fear: Can Predation Risk Structure Ecosystems?" *BioScience* 54, no. 8 (2004): 755.

29. Joel Berger, *The Better to Eat You With: Fear in the Animal World* (Chicago: University of Chicago Press, 2008).

30. Cristina Eisenberg, *The Wolf's Tooth: Keystone Predators, Trophic Cascades, and Biodiversity* (Washington, DC: Island Press, 2011); William Stolzenburg, *Where the Wild Things Were: Life, Death, and Ecological Wreckage in a Land of Vanishing Predators* (New York: Bloomsbury, 2008).

31. Kevin R. Crooks and Michael E. Soulé, "Mesopredator Release and Avifaunal Extinctions in a Fragmented System," *Nature* 400, no. 6744 (1999): 563–66.

32. C. E. Krumm et al., "Mountain Lions Prey Selectively on Prion-Infected Mule Deer," *Biology Letters* 6, no. 2 (October 28, 2009): 209–11.

33. Mark Twain, *Roughing It*, 3rd revised ed., ed. Harriet Elinor Smith et al. (Berkeley: University of California Press, 2011).

34. Gerhard Peters and John T. Woolley, "Richard Nixon: Statement on Signing the Endangered Species Act of 1973," *The American Presidency Project*, n.d., http://www.presidency.ucsb.edu/ws/?pid=4090.

35. "Yellowstone's Popular Alpha Female Wolf Shot Dead by Hunters Outside Park," *Guardian* (UK), December 9, 2012, http://www.theguardian.com/uk/2012/dec/09/yellowstone-female-wolf-dead-hunters.

36. "Wolves 101," Defenders of Wildlife, 10, accessed August 24, 2013, http://www.defenders.org/wolf/wolves-101.

37. "Endangered and Threatened Wildlife and Plants; Removing the Gray Wolf (*Canis lupus*) from the List of Endangered and Threatened Wildlife and Maintaining Protections for the Mexican Wolf (*Canis lupus Baileyi*) by Listing It as Endangered," *Federal Register* 78, no. 114 (June 13, 2013): 35664–719.

38. Phil Taylor of Greenwire, "Wolf Delisting Survives Budget Fight, as Settlement Crumbles," *New York Times*, April 11, 2011; "Budget Bill Rider Will Delist Wolves," *Helena (MT) Independent Record*, April 15, 2011, http://helenair.com.

CHAPTER 3

1. Michael Pollan, *The Omnivore's Dilemma: A Natural History of Four Meals* (New York: Penguin, 2006); Richard Louv, *Last Child in the Woods: Saving Our Children from Nature-Deficit Disorder* (Chapel Hill, NC: Algonquin, 2008).

2. Ibid.

3. Associated Press, "Big Mac Hits the Big 4–0," CBS News, February 11, 2009, http://www.cbsnews.com/.

4. Agricultural Statistics Board, *Cattle Death Loss* (Washington, DC: National Agricultural Statistics Service, Agricultural Statistics Board, US Department of Agriculture, May 12, 2011).

5. Rosamond Naylor and Henning Steinfeld, "Losing the Links Between Livestock and Land," *Science* 1117856, no. 1621 (2005): 310.

6. Ibid.

CHAPTER 4

1. "WildEarth Guardians," *WildEarth Guardians*, accessed September 28, 2013, http://www.wildearthguardians.org/.

2. Sandra M. C. Cavalcanti and Eric M. Gese, "Kill Rates and Predation Patterns of Jaguars (*Panthera onca*) in the Southern Pantanal, Brazil," *Journal of Mammalogy* 91, no. 3 (June 16, 2010): 722–36.

3. Sandra Cavalcanti et al., "Jaguars, Livestock, and People in Brazil: Realities and Perceptions Behind the Conflict" (2010).

4. John Bissonette et al., "Assessment of Costs Associated with Deer–Vehicle Collisions: Human Death and Injury, Vehicle Damage, and Deer Loss," *Human–Wildlife Interactions* (January 1, 2008).

5. Luke Runyon, "Disappearing Mule Deer: A New Reality Throughout Western US," *All Things Considered*, National Public Radio, January 4, 2013.

6. Anis Auoude, "Working Group Takes on Mule Deer," *Wildlife Society News*, December 14, 2012.

7. Richard L. Forstall, *UTAH: Population of Counties by Decennial Census: 1900 to 1990* (Washington, DC: US Bureau of the Census, March 27, 1995).

8. Michael J. Robinson, *Predatory Bureaucracy: The Extermination of Wolves and the Transformation of the West* (Boulder: University Press of Colorado, 2005).

9. Andrew Jenner, "Killer Coyotes: Can Shepherds Protect Their Flocks?" *Modern Farmer*, August 14, 2012.

10. Leah Todd, "Wyoming Predator Management Board Launches First Coyote Bounty Program," *Missoulian* (MT), November 20, 2012.

11. Jenner, "Killer Coyotes."

12. *Rankings and Estimates: Rankings of the States 2012 and Estimates of School Statistics 2013* (NEA Research, December 2012). Coyote removal: Melena Ryzik, "The Sly Coyote Becomes a Bounty Hunters' Target in Utah," *New York Times*, March 22, 2013.

13. Rebecca A. Bartel and Mark W. Brunson, "Effects of Utah's Coyote Bounty Program on Harvester Behavior," *Wildlife Society Bulletin* (2003): 736–43.

14. Mark A. Hurley et al., "Demographic Response of Mule Deer to Experimental Reduction of Coyotes and Mountain Lions in Southeastern Idaho," *Wildlife Monographs* 178, no. 1 (August 2011): 1–33.

15. Ibid.

16. Richard M. Bartmann et al., "Compensatory Mortality in a Colorado Mule Deer Population," *Wildlife Monographs* 121 (1992): 1–39.

17. Ibid.

18. Warren B. Ballard et al., "Deer-Predator Relationships: A Review of Recent North American Studies with Emphasis on Mule and Black-Tailed Deer," *Wildlife Society Bulletin* 29 (2001): 99–115.

19. Ibid.

CHAPTER 5

1. L. David Mech, *The Wolf* (Minneapolis: University of Minnesota Press, 1981); L. David Mech, *The Wolves of Isle Royale—Fauna of the National Parks of the United States* 7 (Washington, DC: US Government Printing Office, 1966).

2. Henryk Okarma and Włodzimierz Jędrzejewski, "Livetrapping Wolves with Nets," *Wildlife Society Bulletin* 25 (1997): 78–82.

3. Marco Musiani and Elisabetta Visalberghi, "Effectiveness of Fladry on Wolves in Captivity," *Wildlife Society Bulletin* 29, no. 1 (April 1, 2001): 91–98.

4. Michael M. Jaeger et al., "Targeting Alphas Can Make Coyote Control More Effective and Socially Acceptable," *California Agriculture* 55 (October 26, 2001): 32–36.

5. Robert B. Wielgus, "Cougar Management," presented at the Wildland Resources Department Seminar, Utah State University, Logan, UT, April 17, 2012.

6. Alex Edward Mettler and John Anthony Shivik, "Dominance and Neophobia in Coyote (*Canis latrans*) Breeding Pairs," *Applied Animal Behaviour Science* 102, nos. 1–2 (January 2007): 85–94.

7. Ibid.

8. "Amtek Pet Behavior Products," *Amtek Pet Behavior Products*, 2012, http://www.amtekpet.com/.

9. John A. Shivik and Daniel J. Martin, "Aversive and Disruptive Stimulus Applications for Managing Predation," *Proceedings of the Wildlife Damage Management Conference* 9 (2001): 111–19.

10. S. B. Linhart et al., "Electronic Frightening Devices for Reducing Coyote Predation on Domestic Sheep: Efficacy Under Range Conditions and Operational Use," *Proceedings of the Vertebrate Pest Conference* 15 (Davis, University of California: 1992): 386–92.

11. Carter Niemeyer, *Wolfer: A Memoir* (Boise, ID: Bottlefly Press, 2012).

12. Ibid.

13. Stewart W. Breck et al., "Non-Lethal Radio Activated Guard for Deterring Wolf Depredation in Idaho: Summary and Call for Research," *Proceedings of the Vertebrate Pest Conference* 20 (Davis: University of California, 2002): 223–26.

14. Ibid.

15. "Yardguard.com—Everything You Need to Guard Your Yard," Yardguard.com, May 9, 2002, http://www.yardguard.com/.

16. Mary Bomford and Peter H. O'Brien, "Sonic Deterrents in Animal Damage Control: A Review of Device Tests and Effectiveness," *Wildlife Society Bulletin* 18, no. 4 (December 1, 1990): 411–22; Helena Bender, "Deterrence of Kangaroos from Agricultural Areas Using Ultrasonic Frequencies: Efficacy of a Commercial Device," *Wildlife Society Bulletin* 31, no. 4 (December 1, 2003): 1037–46.

17. William F. Andelt, "Effectiveness of Livestock Guarding Dogs for Reducing Predation on Domestic Sheep," *Wildlife Society Bulletin* 20, no. 1 (April 1, 1992): 55–62.

18. Jeffrey S. Green et al., "Livestock-Guarding Dogs for Predator Control: Costs, Benefits, and Practicality," *Wildlife Society Bulletin* 12, no. 1 (April 1, 1984): 44–50.

19. Thomas M. Gehring et al., "Livestock Protection Dogs in the 21st Century: Is an Ancient Tool Relevant to Modern Conservation Challenges?" *BioScience* 60 (April 1, 2010): 299–308.

20. Marguerite Holloway, "Wolves at the Door," *Discover*, June 2000.

21. Murray T. Walton and C. Andy Field, "Use of Donkeys to Guard Sheep and Goats in Texas," *Eastern Wildlife Damage Control Conference* 4 (Sun

Prairie, WI: USDA Animal Damage Control, September 25, 1989): 87–94.

22. Laurie E. Meadows and Frederick F. Knowlton, "Efficacy of Guard Llamas to Reduce Canine Predation on Domestic Sheep," *Wildlife Society Bulletin* 28, no. 3 (October 1, 2000): 614–22.

23. "Defenders in Action: Helping Ranchers Coexist with Wolves," Defenders of Wildlife, http://www.defenders.org/northern-rockies-gray-wolf/defenders-action-helping-ranchers-coexist-wolves.

24. Samuel B. Linhart et al., "Komondor Guard Dogs Reduce Sheep Losses to Coyotes: A Preliminary Evaluation," *Journal of Range Management* 32, no. 3 (1979): 238–41.

25. Linhart et al., "Electronic Frightening Devices."

26. D. A. Slate et al., "Decision Making for Wildlife Damage Management," in *Transactions of the North American Wildlife Natural Resources Conference* 57 (Washington, DC: Wildlife Management Institute, 1992), 51–62.

27. Gerald R. Ford, Executive Order 11917—Amending Executive Order No. 11643 of February 8, 1972, Relating to Environmental Safeguards on Activities for Animal Damage Control on Federal Lands, US 41 FR 22239 (1976).

CHAPTER 6

1. Lynne B. Gilbert-Norton et al., "The Effect of Randomly Altering the Time and Location of Feeding on the Behaviour of Captive Coyotes (*Canis Latrans*)," *Applied Animal Behaviour Science* 120, nos. 3–4 (September 2009): 179–85.

2. Lynne B. Gilbert-Norton et al., "Coyotes (*Canis Latrans*) and the Matching Law," *Behavioural Processes* 82, no. 2 (October 2009): 178–83.

3. Patrick Austin Darrow and John Anthony Shivik, "Bold, Shy, and Persistent: Variable Coyote Response to Light and Sound Stimuli," *Applied Animal Behaviour Science* 116, no. 1 (January 2009): 82–87.

4. John A. Shivik et al., "Nonlethal Techniques for Managing Predation: Primary and Secondary Repellents," *Conservation Biology* 17, no. 6 (2003): 1531–37.

5. Mark Twain, *Roughing It*, 3rd revised ed., ed. Harriet Elinor Smith, Edgar Marquess Branch, and Robert Pack Browning (Berkeley: University of California Press, 2011).

6. Lynne B. Gilbert-Norton et al., "The Effect of Social Hierarchy on Captive Coyote (*Canis latrans*) Foraging Behavior," *Ethology* 119, no. 4 (April 2013): 335–43.

7. "Isaac Asimov," Science Fiction-Lit.com, accessed August 31, 2013, http://www.sciencefiction-lit.com/isaac-asimov.html.

8. Gilbert-Norton et al., "The Effect of Social Hierarchy on Captive Coyote (*Canis latrans*) Foraging Behavior."

CHAPTER 7

1. Kari Signor, "Investigating Methods to Reduce Black Bear (*Ursus americanus*) Visitation to Anthropogenic Food Sources: Conditioned Taste Aversion and Food Removal," master's thesis, Utah State University, 2009.

2. J. Garcia et al., "Conditioned Aversion to Saccharin Resulting from Exposure to Gamma Radiation," *Science* 122, no. 3160 (July 22, 1955): 157–58.

3. Carl R. Gustavson et al., "Coyote Predation Control by Aversive Conditioning," *Science* 184, no. 4136 (May 3, 1974): 581–83.

4. Stuart R. Ellins, *Living with Coyotes: Managing Predators Humanely Using Food Aversion Conditioning* (Austin: University of Texas Press, 2005).

5. D.L. Quick et al., "Coyote Control and Taste Aversion," *Appetite* 6, no. 3 (September 1985): 253–64; R.J. Burns and G.E. Connolly, "A Comment on 'Coyote Control and Taste Aversion,'" *Appetite* 6, no. 3 (September 1985): 276–81; D.A. Wade, "Brief Comments on 'Coyote Control and Taste Aversion,'" *Appetite* 6, no. 3 (September 1985): 268–71; S.R. Ellins, "Coyote Control and Taste Aversion: A Predation Problem or a People Problem?" *Appetite* 6, no. 3 (September 1985): 272–75.

6. Ellins, *Living with Coyotes*. Indictments: Lowell K. Nicolaus, "Conditioned Taste Aversion, and the Wildlife Management Hierarchy," www.conditionedtasteaversion.net.

7. J. Garcia et al., "Behavioral Regulation of the Milieu Interne in Man and Rat," *Science* 185, no. 4154 (September 6, 1974): 824–31.

8. Stewart W. Breck et al., "Selective Foraging for Anthropogenic Resources by Black Bears: Minivans in Yosemite National Park," *Journal of Mammalogy* 90, no. 5 (2009): 1041–44.

9. Mark A. Ternent and David L. Garshelis, "Taste-Aversion Conditioning to Reduce Nuisance Activity by Black Bears in a Minnesota Military Reservation," *Wildlife Society Bulletin* (1999): 720–28.

10. Signor, "Investigating Methods to Reduce Black Bear (*Ursus americanus*) Visitation."

11. Nicolaus, "Conditioned Taste Aversion."

12. Ternent and Garshelis, "Taste-Aversion Conditioning."

13. Signor, "Investigating Methods to Reduce Black Bear (*Ursus Americanus*) Visitation."

14. Rachel L. Mazur, "Does Aversive Conditioning Reduce Human–Black Bear Conflict?" *Journal of Wildlife Management* 74, no. 1 (January 2010): 48–54; Jennifer Leigh and Michael Chamberlain, "Effects of Aversive Conditioning on Behavior of Nuisance Louisiana Black Bears," *Human–Wildlife Conflicts* 2 (January 1, 2008): 175–82.

15. John A. Shivik et al., "Electronic Aversive Conditioning for Managing

Wolf Predation," *Proceedings: Vertebrate Pest Conference* 20 (Davis: University of California, 2002): 227–31.

16. William F. Andelt et al., "Coyote Predation on Domestic Sheep Deterred with Electronic Dog-Training Collar," *Wildlife Society Bulletin* 27, no. 1 (April 1, 1999): 12–18.

17. S.B. Linhart et al., "Electronic Frightening Devices for Reducing Coyote Predation on Domestic Sheep: Efficacy Under Range Conditions and Operational Use," *Proceedings of the Vertebrate Pest Conference* 15 (1992): 386–92.

18. Jason E. Hawley et al., "Assessment of Shock Collars as Nonlethal Management for Wolves in Wisconsin," *Journal of Wildlife Management* 73, no. 4 (May 2009): 518–25.

19. Ibid.

20. Nathan Lance, "Application of Electrified Fladry to Decrease Risk of Livestock Depredations by Wolves (*Canis lupus*)," master's thesis, Utah State University, 2009, http://digitalcommons.usu.edu/etd/282.

21. N.J. Lance et al., "Biological, Technical, and Social Aspects of Applying Electrified Fladry for Livestock Protection from Wolves (*Canis lupus*)," *Wildlife Research* 37, no. 8 (2010): 708–14.

CHAPTER 8

1. Peter Langdon Bird, *Management of Dingoes in South Australia* (Adelaide: Government of South Australia, 2010); *Policy on Management of Dingo Populations* (Adelaide: Government of South Australia, 2011).

2. Mordecai O. Ogada et al., "Livestock Depredation by African Carnivores: The Role of Livestock Husbandry," *Conservation Biology* 17, no. 6 (2003): 1521–30.

3. James T. Jardine, *Coyote-Proof Pasture Experiment, 1908* (Washington, DC: Government Printing Office, 1909).

4. Jonathan S. Adams, *The Future of the Wild: Radical Conservation for a Crowded World* (Boston: Beacon Press, 2006).

5. Michael L. Rosenzweig, *Win-Win Ecology: How the Earth's Species Can Survive in the Midst of Human Enterprise* (New York: Oxford University Press, 2003).

6. James R. Miller and Richard J. Hobbs, "Conservation Where People Live and Work," *Conservation Biology* 16, no. 2 (2002): 330–37.

7. Ogada et al., "Livestock Depredation by African Carnivores"; John A. Shivik et al., "Nonlethal Techniques for Managing Predation: Primary and Secondary Repellents," *Conservation Biology* 17, no. 6 (2003): 1531–37.

8. Ogada et al., "Livestock Depredation by African Carnivores."

9. Lynne B. Gilbert-Norton et al., "The Effect of Randomly Altering the Time and Location of Feeding on the Behaviour of Captive Coyotes

(*Canis latrans*)," *Applied Animal Behaviour Science* 120, nos. 3–4 (September 2009): 179–85.

10. Julie K. Young et al., "Does Spatial Structure Persist Despite Resource and Population Changes? Effects of Experimental Manipulations on Coyotes," *Journal of Mammalogy* 89, no. 5 (2008): 1094–104.

11. J. K. Young et al., "A Comparison of Coyote Ecology after 25 Years: 1978 Versus 2003," *Canadian Journal of Zoology* 84 (2006): 573–82.

12. Gordon C. Haber, "Biological, Conservation, and Ethical Implications of Exploiting and Controlling Wolves," *Conservation Biology* 10, no. 4 (1996): 1068–81.

13. Michael M. Jaeger et al., "Targeting Alphas Can Make Coyote Control More Effective and Socially Acceptable," *California Agriculture* 55 (October 26, 2001): 32–36.

14. Mary M. Conner et al., "Effect of Coyote Removal on Sheep Depredation in Northern California," *Journal of Wildlife Management* 62, no. 2 (April 1, 1998): 690–99, doi:10.2307/3802345.

15. Jaeger et al., "Targeting Alphas."

16. Karen M. Blejwas et al., "The Effectiveness of Selective Removal of Breeding Coyotes in Reducing Sheep Predation," *Journal of Wildlife Management* 66, no. 2 (April 1, 2002): 451–62, doi:10.2307/3803178.

17. Farley Mowat, *Never Cry Wolf* (Boston: Little, Brown, 1963).

18. John A. Shivik et al., "Will an Artificial Scent Boundary Prevent Coyote Intrusion?" *Wildlife Society Bulletin* 35, no. 4 (2011): 494–97.

19. James A. Till and Frederick F. Knowlton, "Efficacy of Denning in Alleviating Coyote Depredations Upon Domestic Sheep," *Journal of Wildlife Management* 47, no. 4 (October 1, 1983): 1018–25.

20. C. E. Spence et al., "Surgical Sterilization of Free-Ranging Wolves," *Canadian Veterinary Journal* 40, no. 2 (February 1999): 118–21.

21. Tim Mowry, "Sterilized Wolves Seem to Live Longer in the Wild," *Alaska Fish and Wildlife News* (Juneau: Alaska Department of Fish and Game, May 2004) http://www.adfg.alaska.gov/.

22. Cassity Bromley and Eric M. Gese, "Effects of Sterilization on Territory Fidelity and Maintenance, Pair Bonds, and Survival Rates of Free-ranging Coyotes," *Canadian Journal of Zoology* 79 (February 26, 2001): 386–92; Cassity Bromley and Eric M. Gese, "Surgical Sterilization as a Method of Reducing Coyote Predation on Domestic Sheep," *Journal of Wildlife Management* 65 (July 1, 2001): 510–19.

23. George A. Feldhamer, Bruce Carlyle Thompson, and Joseph A. Chapman, *Wild Mammals of North America: Biology, Management, and Conservation* (Baltimore: Johns Hopkins University Press, 2003).

24. David L. Garshelis et al., "Landowners' Perceptions of Crop Damage and Management Practices Related to Black Bears in East-Central Minnesota," *Ursus* 11 (January 1, 1999): 219–24.

25. Christopher Ketcham, "America's Secret War on Wildlife," *Men's Journal*, January 2008.

26. J. Shivik et al., "Are the Same Bears Repeatedly Translocated from Corn Crops in Wisconsin?" *Ursus* 22 (January 1, 2011): 114–19.

27. Ibid.

CHAPTER 9

1. Eric M. Gese et al., "Effectiveness of Theobromine and Caffeine Mixtures in Coyote Lure Operative Devices as a Predacide: A Simulated Field Study," *Sheep and Goat Research Journal* 27 (2012): 26–31.

2. National Research Council, "Changes in the Sheep Industry in the United States" (Washington, DC: National Academy of Sciences, 2008).

3. US Department of Agriculture, *USDA Economic Research Service—Trade*, May 26, 2012, http://www.ers.usda.gov/topics/animal-products/sheep, -lamb-mutton/trade.aspx#.Uin9a8b92uJ.

4. Peter Langdon Bird, *Management of Dingoes in South Australia* (Adelaide: Government of South Australia, 2010).

5. Karyn Moskowitz and Chuck Romaniello, *Assessing the Full Cost of the Federal Grazing Program* (Tucson, AZ: Center for Biological Diversity, 2002).

6. Rosamond Naylor et al., "Losing the Links Between Livestock and Land," *Science* 1117856, no. 1621 (2005): 310.

7. J.L. Capper, "The Environmental Impact of Beef Production in the United States: 1977 Compared with 2007," *Journal of Animal Science* 89, no. 12 (July 29, 2011): 4249–61, doi:10.2527/jas.2010–3784.

8. John A. Shivik et al., "Nonlethal Techniques for Managing Predation: Primary and Secondary Repellents," *Conservation Biology* 17, no. 6 (2003): 1531–37; Eric Gese, Sean Keenan, and Ann Kitchen, *Lines of Defense: Coping with Predators in the Rocky Mountain Region* (Logan: Utah State University Extension, 2005); Suzanne Asha Stone et al., *Livestock and Wolves: A Guide to Nonlethal Tools and Methods to Reduce Conflicts* (Washington, DC: Defenders of Wildlife, 2008); John A. Shivik, "Tools for the Edge: What's New for Conserving Carnivores," *BioScience* 56, no. 3 (2006): 253–59.

9. J. Russell Mason and Richard J. Burns, "Effectiveness of Vichos Non-Lethal Collars in Deterring Coyote Attacks on Sheep," *Proceedings of the Vertebrate Pest Conference* 17 (Davis: University of California at Davis, 1992), 204–6.

10. Vernen Liles, "Sheep Wars," June 15, 2010, Texas State Historical Society, http://www.tshaonline.org/handbook/online/articles/azs01.

11. D.M. Anderson et al., "Managing Livestock Using Animal Behavior: Mixed-species Stocking and Flerds," *Animal* 6, no. 8 (February 10, 2012): 1339–49.

12. Patrick Crowley et al., "Roadkill Composting in Montana. A Seasonal Rotation Approach," Montana Department of Environmental Quality, 2006.

13. Seth Wilson, "Livestock Carcass Removal and Composting," *Home Range* (Summer 2007), http://www.keystoneconservation.us/keystone_conservation/files/home_range_S07.pdf, accessed May 15, 2013.

14. Philip J. Nyhus et al., "Taking the Bite Out of Wildlife Damage: The Challenges of Wildlife Compensation Schemes," *Conservation Magazine* 4, no. 2 (2003): 37–40.

15. Lisa Naughton-Treves et al., "Paying for Tolerance: Rural Citizens' Attitudes Toward Wolf Depredation and Compensation," *Conservation Biology* 17, no. 6 (2003): 1500–1511.

16. "Defenders of Wildlife Financial Statements and Independent Auditors' Report, September 30, 2011 and 2010," Rogers & Company, PLLC, Certified Public Accountants, February 2012.

17. Abigail Breuer, author phone interview, January 31, 2012.

18. "Wildlife Friendly Producers," Wildlife Friendly Enterprise Network, http://wildlifefriendly.org/products/northamericanproducers/.

CHAPTER 10

1. Peter Matthiessen, *The Snow Leopard* (New York: Bantam, 1981).

2. M.D. Jimenez and S.A. Becker, eds., *Northern Rocky Mountain Wolf Recovery Program 2012 Interagency Annual Report* (Helena, MT: USFWS, Ecological Services, 2013).

3. Mary Ann Bonnell, author phone interview, April 22, 2013.

4. "Coyote Hazing: An Effective Tool for Shaping Coyote Behavior," City of Aurora (CO) Parks, Recreation, and Open Space, 2012; *How to Haze a Coyote*, 2013, YouTube.com.

5. Stephen Herrero et al., "Fatal Attacks by American Black Bear on People: 1900–2009," *Journal of Wildlife Management* 75, no. 3 (2011): 596–603.

6. Dave Smith, *Don't Get Eaten: The Dangers of Animals That Charge or Attack* (Seattle: Mountaineers Books, 2003).

7. Herrero et al., "Fatal Attacks by American Black Bear on People."

8. Smith, *Don't Get Eaten.*

9. Tom S. Smith et al., "Efficacy of Firearms for Bear Deterrence in Alaska," *Journal of Wildlife Management* 76, no. 5 (2012): 1021–27.

10. Interagency Grizzly Bear Executive Committee, "IGBC Bear Spray Recommendations," 2008, http://www.igbconline.org/.

11. Kathy Etling, *Cougar Attacks: Encounters of the Worst Kind*, 1st ed. (Guilford, CT: Lyons Press, 2004); Smith, *Don't Get Eaten.*

12. George Janson, "Jaryd Atadero Search: A Second Look," *Colorado Search and Rescue Board Newsletter* (Colorado Springs: Colorado Search and Rescue Board, July 2003).

13. Etling, *Cougar Attacks.*

14. Kevin M. Kadesky et al., "Cougar Attacks on Children: Injury Patterns and Treatment," *Journal of Pediatric Surgery* 33, no. 6 (June 1998): 863–65.

15. Mark E. McNay, *A Case History of Human-Wolf Encounters in Alaska and Canada* (Alaska Department of Fish and Game, 2002).

16. *Wisconsin Wolf Regulations 2013* (Wisconsin Department of Natural Resources, 2013).

17. Wisconsin Wolf Advisory Committee, *Wisconsin Wolf Management Plan* (Wisconsin Department of Natural Resources, 1999).

18. T. Horiuchi et al., "Ketamine Lollipop for Pediatric Premedication," *Masui: The Japanese Journal of Anesthesiology* 50, no. 4 (April 2001): 410–12.

19. Keith G. Rasmussen et al., "Serial Infusions of Low-Dose Ketamine for Major Depression," *Journal of Psychopharmacology* 27, no. 5 (May 1, 2013): 444–50.

20. Jackie Dawson et al., "The Carbon Cost of Polar Bear Viewing Tourism in Churchill, Canada," *Journal of Sustainable Tourism* 18, no. 3 (2010): 319–36; Zac Unger, *Never Look a Polar Bear in the Eye: A Family Field Trip to the Arctic's Edge in Search of Adventure, Truth, and Mini-Marshmallows* (Philadelphia: Del Capo, 2013).

INDEX

aerial hunting, 9
Andelt, Bill, 115, 124
Animal and Plant Health Inspection
 Service (APHIS), 12
animal armor, 138
Animal Damage Control Act
 (ADC), 11, 12
animal husbandry: altering the
 timing of breeding, 139;
 animal armor use, 138; carcass
 collection and composting,
 139; history of the sheep
 industry in the US, 134–35;
 human need for animal protein,
 136; livestock compensation
 program, 140–41; mixing
 sheep and cattle herds as a
 deterrence, 139; night penning
 of cattle, 140; "Predator
 Friendly" concept, 142–45;
 question of how to balance
 human and biological systems,
 136–38; ranchers' connection
 to the land, 135–36; ranchers'
 reaction to compensation
 programs, 141
Animal Welfare Act, 12
APHIS (Animal and Plant Health
 Inspection Service), 12

Asher, Val, 111–15, 161
Ataderyo, Jaryd, 157–58
aversive stimuli: behavioral
 conditioning studies, 108–9;
 challenges of, 111; CTA
 experiment setup, 102–3; CTA
 field experiment results, 105–7;
 CTA one-trial effectiveness,
 104; CTA reliability, 107–8;
 CTA scale-up problems, 103–4;
 electrified fladry experiment
 with wolves, 117–19; evidence
 that bears learn and remember,
 110; process of conditioning
 an animal, 110–11; ranchers'
 resistance to costs, 119–20;
 shock collar experimental
 setup, 112–13; shock collar
 scale-up to field conditions,
 115–16; unexpected result of
 an experimental control setup,
 113–14, 117; wolves' reaction to
 a shock collar, 114–15
Avian Systems, 81–82
Aztecs, 7

Bangs, Ed, 140, 166, 170
Baron, David, 33–34
bears (*Ursus*): adaptations to food

sources, 131; black (*see* black
bears); brown (*see* grizzly bears);
damage done to food crops,
130, 131; fladry's affect on, 97;
liability questions regarding
human deaths from, 31–32;
personality differences between
species, 96–98; polar bears in
Manitoba, 166–68; translocation
program in Wisconsin, 131–33
bear spray, 156
Beast in the Garden, The (Baron),
33–34
Beckel, Mark, 53
behavioral conditioning studies,
108–9
Berger, Kim, 135
bio-boundaries experiments,
126–27
black bears: annual damage done by,
104–5; attraction to minivans,
105; CTA experiment setup,
102–3; CTA field experiment
results, 105–7; dangers to
children from, 154, 155;
dangers to humans from,
30–31, 153–54; evidence that
bears learn and remember,
110; pattern of attacks, 153–54;
process of conditioning, 110–
11; recommended response to
presence of, 153–55
Blackfoot Challenge, 139
bobcats, 9
Bonnell, Mary Ann, 150, 159–60
bounties to protect deer
populations, 63, 66
Bourassa, Gene, 79
Boyd, Diane, 27, 28, 29
Branch of Economic Ornithology
and Mammalogy, USDA, 10
Brazil, 60–61
Breck, Stewart, 105

breeding times alterations, 139
Breuer, Abigail, 142–43, 144
Bromley, Cass, 128–29
brown bears. *See* grizzly bears
Bureau of Biological Survey, US, 10
Busby, Fee, 14

Cain Report, 11
Callahan, Peggy, 51–52, 53
Canis latrans. *See* coyotes
Canis lupus. *See* wolves
carcass collection and composting,
139
Cavalcanti, Sandra, 60–61
Center for Biological Diversity,
136
Center for Environmental Science
and Policy, 44
Certified Wildlife Friendly, 143–44
chronic wasting disease, 37
Churchill, Manitoba, 166–68
classical conditioning, 108
Collarum, 57, 60
compensatory mortality, 64
Compound 1080, 10, 135
conditioned taste aversion (CTA):
field experiment results, 105–7;
reliability of, 107–8; scale-up
problems, 103–4; setup for an
experiment, 102–3
Connolly, Guy, 13, 65–66
cougars (mountain lions):
arguments about the dangers
of, 33–34; dangers to children
from, 157–59; indirect effects on
the ecosystem, 37; population
expansion, 33; predation rate,
33; protected species status,
32–33; recommended response
to presence of, 158–59
coyotes (*Canis latrans*): ability
to predict food locations,
89; ability to survive in the

suburbs, 21–22; aerial hunting's effectiveness against, 9; attacks on people, 22; bio-boundaries experiments on, 126–27; cattle kills, 26; a coyote's relationship with a researcher, 94–95; Critter Gitter experiment with, 75–76; effectiveness of predator control for game protection, 63–64; emotional responses to, 30; encounter with a researcher, 21, 23; fladry research project, 73–74; a former farmer's perspective on, 47; human assumption of a right to dominate, 13–14; idea of a personality, 95; impact of bounty programs in Utah, 63; indirect effects on the ecosystem, 37; investigation into removing specific animals, 124–25; investigation of their territorial behavior, 123–24; legends and stories about, 7–8; link between food availability and behavior, 90–91; observations of personalities in the animals, 91–93, 95, 146; pack reaction to an alarm, 95–96; parallels between some human and predator behaviors, 98–99; population distribution in America, 6–7; predation on pets, 22; reproductive rate, 13; research using automatic feeders, 90; scale of predator control needed to impact populations, 65–66; sheep losses to predation, 8; sizes of, 7; social context test lessons learned, 99–101; sterilization hypothesis and program, 128–30

Critter Gitter, 74–76
CTA. *See* conditioned taste aversion (CTA).
Cummings, Edward, 78, 137, 140

Darrow, Patrick, 45–47, 93–96, 142, 147
deer: calls for bounties to reduce deer predator populations, 63, 66; chronic wasting disease and, 37; perception of a decrease in populations, 62; reality of dangers to humans from deer populations, 62
Defenders of Wildlife, 28, 86–87, 140, 149
Department of Natural Resources, Wisconsin, 141
Deseret Ranch, 128
disruptive stimuli: animal-activated alarms efficacy, 74–75; behavior-contingent activation of a repellant, 76; components of the best devices, 84–85; Critter Gitter experiment with coyotes, 75–76; fladry research, 70–74; force multiplier present after lethal removals, 73–74; guard dogs use, 85–86; humans as guard animals, 86–87; MAG's affect on varied species, 97–98; predators' ability to adapt to stimuli, 77–78; premise of, 69, 70; radio-collar-activated siren's efficacy, 79–80; RAG box use, 81–83; ultrasonic sound's use, 83–84; Wildlife Services' preference for lethal methods, 87–88
Division of Biological Survey, (USDA), 10
Division of Ornithology and Mammalogy, (USDA), 10

Division of Predatory Animal and
　Rodent Control (PARC), 10–11
Domínguez, Francisco García, 57
donkeys, as guard animals, 86

Earth Day, 4
Electronic Guard, 79
Elephant Pepper, 144
elk, 36, 47–49
Endangered Species Act (1973), 4,
　11, 12, 39, 40
Eradication Methods Laboratory,
　New Mexico, 11

Federal Aid in Wildlife Restoration
　Act (1937), 65
fences as deterrents, 121–22
feral hogs, 9
Fish and Wildlife Services, (US),
　12, 40
fladry: dominant and subordinate
　coyotes' reactions to, 74; effect
　on bears, 97; experiment with
　electrified fladry, 117–19;
　invention by hunters,
　70–71; research on optimum
　arrangement, 72–73; research
　project involving coyotes,
　73–74; used to capture wolves,
　71–72
flerds, 139
food production: cost of predation,
　43; disconnect between
　consumers and food sources,
　50; efficiency of modern protein
　production, 44–45; experience
　of hunting and preparing
　your own meat, 47–50;
　human manipulation of the
　environment for, 45; livestock
　requirements of the mechanized
　food industry, 44; problem of
　predators jeopardizing open
　food production systems, 45;

variety and quantity of food
　in America, 42–43; views on
　the utility of mass-production
　means, 49
foxes, 9, 57

Garcia, John, 103
Gese, Eric, 21, 129
Gilbert-Norton, Lynne: addition
　of social context into her
　research, 99–101; bio-
　boundaries experiments on
　coyotes, 126–27; encounter
　with coyotes, 23; entry into
　coyote pen, 19–21; observations
　of animal personalities, 91–93,
　146; questions for her research,
　18–19; reaction to America, 18,
　42; research on coyote behavior
　around food, 90–91; start of
　study of coyotes, 5; work at the
　facility, 98
golden jackal, 8
grizzly bears (*Ursus arctos*):
　behavior and habitats, 155;
　on the California state flag,
　43; population decimation, 4,
　31; recommended response to
　presence of, 155–56; threat to
　humans, 31
guard dogs, 85–87

Hawley, Jason, 115–16
Herrero, Stephen, 153, 154
Hopland Research and Extension
　Center, California, 124–25
human-wildland interface:
　attraction of human habitats
　to animals, 16, 21; coyotes'
　ability to survive in the suburbs,
　21–22; landscape design
　that contributes to interface
　problems, 159–61; myth about a
　problem of proximity of humans

and predators, 123; porous
nature of, 3

Interagency Grizzly Bear
Committee, 156
Ives, Samuel, 31–32

Jaeger, Mike, 124–25
jaguars, 60–61
Jędrzejewski, Włodzimierz, 71
Jimenez, Mike, 27

Keefover-Ring, Wendy, 33–34
Keystone Conservation, 143
King Collar, 138
Knowlton, Fred, 14–15, 127

Lancaster, Scott, 33–34
Lance, Nathan, 117–20
Leopold, Aldo, 11, 161
Leopold, A. Starker, 11
Leopold Report, 11
Linhart, Sam, 115
livestock compensation program,
140–41
llamas as guard animals, 86
Lorenz, Konrad, 108

M-44 cyanide ejector, 88
MAG (Movement Activated
Guard), 97–98
Manitoba Conservation, 167–68
Martin, Kerry, 96
Matarranz, Victor García, 57
McNay, Mark, 159
Mech, David, 52, 69
Mettler, Alex, 73, 74, 98, 99
Migratory Bird Treaty Act, 11
Mock, Karen, 132
Montana Wildlife Services, 28
mountain lions (*Puma concolor*):
arguments about the dangers
of, 33–34; dangers to children
from, 157–59; indirect effects on

the ecosystem, 37; population
expansion, 33; predation rate,
33; protected species status,
32–33; recommended response
to presence of, 158–59
Movement Activated Guard
(MAG), 97–98
Mule Deer Protection Act, 63
Musiani, Marco, 72

National Agricultural Statistics
Service, 8, 25
Native Americans, 7
Naylor, Rosamond, 44
Niemeyer, Carter, 79, 80
night penning, 140
Nixon, Richard, 9–10, 39

Ogada, Mordecai, 122
Okarma, Henryk, 71
operant conditioning, 108
Oregon State University, 36

Packard, Jane, 52
PARC (Division of Predatory
Animal and Rodent Control),
10–11
Pavlov, Ivan, 108
perception-blight hypothesis, 61
personality of animals: coyote's
relationship with researcher,
94–95; idea of wild animals
having a personality, 95;
observations of personalities in
coyotes, 91–93, 146; parallels
between some human and
predator behaviors, 98–99;
social context of, in reactions to
food, 99–101; wolves, 113–14,
117–18
Peterson, Andy, 150
Pittman-Robertson act, 65
Polar Bear Alert Program, 167–68
polar bears, 166–68

Polish Academy of Sciences, 71
Predator Conservation Alliance, 143
"Predator Friendly" concept, 142, 145; creation of a new label, 143–44; difficulty attracting followers, 142–43; example of a successful model, 144; growth in the label, 144–45; marketing power of the label, 144
Predator Research Facility: Critter Gitter experiment with coyotes, 75; facility tour, 14–18; fladry research project, 73–74; focus of current research, 17–18; location, 6; Spaniards' visit, 57
prions, 37
Proposition 117 (California), 32
Psychology Institute, Rome, 72
puma. *See* mountain lions

Quammen, David, 13

Radio Activated Guard (RAG), 79–80, 81–82
Ranglack, Dustin, 102–3
red fox, 9
Ripple, Bill, 36
Rocky Mountain Wolf Recovery Conference, 28
Ruffatto, Tom, 78, 79, 85–86
Ruid, Dave, 130

sanitation effect of cougars, 37
Schultz, Ron, 116
Seal, Ulysses, 52
Section of Predator and Rodent Control, 11
Servicio de Especies Amenazadas (Threatened Species Service, Spain), 57
sheep industry: estimates of losses to predation, 8; history of the industry in the US, 134–35;
mixing sheep and cattle herds, 139; origins of, 8; ranchers' desire to preserve their way of life, 135–36
she-wolf 832F, 40
shock collars: experimental setup with wolves, 112–13; scale-up to field conditions with wolves, 115–16; tragic result of an attempt to manage coexistence, 163–66; wolves' reaction to, 114–15
Signor, Kari, 102, 105–7
Silent Spring, 4
Sinapu, 34
Skinner, B. F., 108
SMART advice, 152, 153
Smith, Tom, 156
Spain, predator management in, 56–60
sterilization program: economic value of, 128–29; hypothesis about the kill instinct of sterilized coyotes, 128–29; ranchers' reaction to, 129–30
Stone, Suzanne, 28
strychnine, 10

territorial behavior of coyotes, 123–24
Tester, Jon, 40
Thinking Like a Mountain (Leopold), 161
Till, James, 127
Tinbergen, Niko, 108
translocation program, 132–33
trophic cascade, 36–37, 40
Turner Endangered Species Fund, 112

ultrasonic sound-based guards, 83–84
United States Department of Agriculture (USDA), 9

University of Montana, 27
Ursus. See bears
Ursus arctos. See grizzly bears
US Fish and Wildlife Service, 12,
    40
Utah, 3–4, 43, 63
Utah State University, 6, 14 ,15,
    46, 132

Vancouver Ministry of
    Environment, Lands, and Parks
    (Canada), 22
Vendergon, Arion, 24, 25
Vichos anti-predator collar, 138
Visalberghi, Elisabetta, 72

Walmart, 142
Welder Wildlife Refuge, Texas,
    123–24
Wildlife Conservation Society, 135
Wildlife Friendly (organization),
    142
Wildlife Science Center,
    Minnesota, 52
Wildlife Services: aerial hunting's
    use to kill coyotes, 9;
    background of current system
    of federal predator control,
    10–11; collateral damage, 12;
    death toll, 12; investigations
    into the agency, 11–12; methods
    of predatory management, 12;
    name origin, 11, 12; past use of
    poisons to manage populations,
    10; preference for lethal
    methods, 87–88; translocation
    program for bears, 131–32
Williamson, Rick, 80, 81
Wilson, Ryan, 125–27
Wilson, Seth, 139
Wisconsin: compensation program,
    141; research into predations
    of cattle and sheep, 24–25;
    translocation program for

bears, 131–32; zones for
    wolves, 161
Wolf Ecology Project, University
    of Montana, 27
wolves (*Canis lupus*): addressing
    denials of threats to humans
    from, 28–29; apparent dislike
    of humans, 70; aversive stimuli
    experimental setup, 112–13;
    balancing management with
    emotional responses, 163,
    164–66; chain of events in
    the predator process, 69–70;
    death toll from aerial hunting,
    9; decimation of the popula-
    tion, 4; documented attacks
    and kills of humans, 29;
    early studies of live animals,
    52–53; ecological significance
    of expansion in the western
    US, 35–37; efforts needed
    to collar a family, 162–64;
    electrified fladry experiment,
    117–19; elimination of in
    other countries, 10; emotional
    responses to, 4, 27, 30, 55–56,
    161–62; experimental shock
    collar setup, 112–13; fladry
    invention, 70–71; management
    zones, 161; number of domestic
    animals killed by, 26; personality
    of, 118; possible infiltration
    into Utah, 4; reaction to a
    shock collar, 114–15; reaction
    to the RAG box, 81–83;
    recommended response to
    presence of, 159; repopulation
    of in North America, 35,
    40; research into predations
    of cattle and sheep, 24–26;
    shock collar scale-up to field
    conditions, 115–16; symbolism
    of, 27, 28; teen Wildlife Center
    visitors' reaction to, 53–55;

tragic result of an attempt to
manage co-existence, 163–66;
unexpected result of an aversive
stimuli experiment, 113–14, 117

YardGuard, 83–84

Yellowstone National Park: grizzly
bears in, 31, 62; repopulation of
wolves in, 34–36
Young, Julie, 123–24

zoning to deter predators, 161

WITHDRAWN